Douglas Wynne

**Let the world know:
#IGotMyCLPBook!**

**Crystal Lake Publishing
www.CrystalLakePub.com**

WELCOME
TO ANOTHER

CRYSTAL LAKE PUBLISHING
CREATION

WELCOME TO ANOTHER CRYSTAL LAKE PUBLISHING CREATION.

Thank you for supporting independent publishing and small presses. You rock, and hopefully you'll quickly realize why we've become one of the world's leading publishers of Dark Fiction and Horror. We have some of the world's best fans for a reason, and hopefully we'll be able to add you to that list really soon.

To follow us behind the scenes (while supporting independent publishing and our authors), be sure to join our interactive community of authors and readers on Patreon (https://www.patreon.com/CLP) for exclusive content. You can even subscribe to all our future releases. Otherwise drop by our website and online store (www.crystallakepub.com/). We'd love to have you.

Welcome to Crystal Lake Publishing—Tales from the Darkest Depths.

For Sue Little, wise woman and bookstore warrior

When peacocks roam through the jungle of virulent poison, though the gardens of medicinal plants may be attractive, the peacock flocks will not take delight in them; for peacocks thrive on the essence of virulent poison.

Likewise when heroes enter the jungle of cyclic existence, though the gardens of happiness and prosperity may seem beautiful, the heroes will not become attached to them; for heroes thrive in the forest of suffering.

–*The Wheel of Sharp Weapons*, Dharmaraksita

New York City, 1991

ON MY WAY back from the one hour photo with a satchel full of sins, I stand on the corner and wait for the dragon to pass before crossing the street. It's my third Chinese New Year in the office on Mott Street where, in spite of spotty work, I haven't been evicted yet, and that dragon is still as impressive as the first time I saw it. Wild-eyed, with curling horns and fierce paper jaws, the silk body winds down the street atop poles held by red and yellow clad dancers. I cross, trot up the steps to my building, and enter the lobby, dripping confetti from my shoes and shoulders. It's a three-story walk-up, my office on the third floor, and by the time I get to the second landing I can hear my phone jangling. That's the sound of thunder in the desert. I quicken my step.

My shoes squeak on the grimy tile floor as I make the turn at the head of the stairs. Dim sunlight filters in through a skylight dome the color of sour milk but doesn't quite reach the end of the corridor where my office sits—the last of four. The fluorescent tubes are dead at my end of the hall. I slot my key into the doorknob by the scant illumination spilling through the frosted glass window in the door, stenciled with gold letters: INSIGHT DETECTIVE AGENCY—MILES LANDRY, PI.

The doors I passed on the way to mine were quiet except for a faint TV at the far end of the hall. I'm guessing my nearest neighbors, the tax accountant and the podiatrist, got out from under the parade while they could, knowing what kind of crimp it would put in business today. The sounds of the street swell up again as I open the door—loud enough that I half expect to see the curtains blowing in the wind from a wide open window to the fire escape. The sound is pouring in through the same gaps in the frame that let the heat out all winter, but the ringing phone is the loudest thing in the room, the hammer trilling on the bell hard enough to almost make it hop off my desk. It's on the third ring when I get through the door and I'm afraid there won't be a fourth.

I leave my keychain hanging from the doorknob, and I'm about to make a lunge for the phone when I get a little assistance from a kick in the ass that sends me sprawling face first on the red oriental carpet in front of my desk.

My valise lands under me, cushioning my fall, and I struggle to disentangle my head from the shoulder strap as I turn to face my attacker. The motion puts my forearm in range of the second kick—no doubt aimed at my jaw. My arm blocks the kick by dumb luck, but recoils, and I hit myself in the face with the back of my own hand.

Blinking through the stinging pain, I make out a female form settling gracefully into a ready stance.

Shit. Sophie Cheung. She looks a lot taller from down here.

I had trailed her for a couple of weeks on behalf of her husband before letting a wiretap on their home phone finish the job. You could say I verified Mr. Cheung's hunch that the karate dojo in alphabet city wasn't the only place where she was breaking a sweat with a fellow instructor. Sophie holds a third-degree black belt.

I wonder if my arm just fractured along the old fault lines.

"How does it feel?" she asks, and I think she means my arm until she says, "Finding out you've been stalked by someone you didn't know was there?" She steps into the room and casually knocks a potted spider plant off an end table with a flick of her hand. The terra cotta pot smashes when it hits the floor, spilling black soil onto the carpet beside me. "How does it feel having *your* private space invaded?"

Okay, that pisses me off. The plant has sentimental value. I know I should be afraid of Sophie from this vulnerable vantage point, but the heat is already flushing my cheeks—a sure sign that I'm unlikely to act in my own best interest for the next little while.

Incredibly, the phone is still ringing. Seems like the answering machine should have clicked on by now, but I've lost count, what with getting my ass kicked and all. The machine is probably broken for good. I don't hit women, but I think I might be tempted if I miss this phone call. Sophie's husband paid me a decent sum, but not enough to compensate for the loss of the *next* job. Or a hospital bill.

"What's in the bag, Landry?" Sophie asks, and sweeps a model airplane off the bookshelf before crunching it underfoot. "Pictures of your latest marks?"

I'm on my feet now, steadying myself with a hand on the desk. It's a cheap particle board jobbie. Fake oak laminate. Wide enough to put me out of range, but I doubt I can get behind it in time if she strikes again.

"I've been following you ever since Rick dropped this divorce crap on me. First thing I find out is that your friends at the bar call you Dirty Laundry. Nice." She looks around the office like she's trying to decide what to break next. She catches me looking at the answering machine. "You messed with my phone, maybe I mess with yours, yeah?"

"Hey," I say, "I'll press charges for assault and destruction of property."

Her eyes lock on mine again and there's new fire in them. I don't know if it's the thought of me adding to her mounting legal fees, but I can tell that with the deep breath she's taking, she's gearing up to close the distance between us.

My face is stinging and the phone is still ringing when I drop my ass onto the desk, swing my legs over, and roll off the other side, sending my office chair skittering away on its wheels. Sophie Cheung shuffles forward, throws her right leg up above her head, and with an inarticulate war cry brings her heel down in an ax kick that breaks the desk clean in half.

As the phone slides down the V toward the break, I snatch the handset out of the cradle. The bottom right drawer rolls open as the desk collapses, and I snatch my gun from it with my free hand, rise and point it at her. "Insight Detective Agency, Miles Landry speaking."

At the sight of the weapon, Sophie slips out the door.

The man on the line has a strong accent. Not Chinese but in the neighborhood.

"Sorry, could you repeat that?" I say, trying not to breathe too hard into the mouthpiece while my galloping heart settles down.

"Mr. Landry? My name is Geshe Norbu. Am I reaching you at a good time?"

I catch my breath. "Just another day in paradise."

"Good, good."

"How can I help you, Mr. Norbu?"

"I'm calling from the Diamond Path Dharma Center in Union Square."

"The what?"

"It's a center for Buddhist studies."

"A Buddhist temple?"

"Yes. We serve the immigrant community of Tibetan refugees and offer free meditation instruction for all."

A religious fundraiser call for Asian refugees. I fought my way to the phone for this?

"I'm calling on behalf of my teacher, Jigme Rinpoche. He would like to consult with you regarding your services."

"My services. As a private eye . . . " I want to make sure this guy called the right number.

"Yes, of course. He is very eager to meet with you."

"Okay, sure," I say, crouching behind the wreckage of my desk with the phone in the crook of my neck, then setting my gun down on the floor to root around for a pen. My desk blotter with the giant calendar page is a shambles of ruffled paper, but I can still write on it if this doesn't turn out to be a scam or a misunderstanding in the next two minutes.

"What kind of job are we talking about? I usually follow people around and catch them up to no good. I thought you guys were the trusting sort."

The monk laughs. Even through a telephone, it sounds more genuine and delighted than most of the laughter I've heard since before boot camp. "Very good," Norbu says. "You know something about Tibetan monks?"

"Not much. Saffron robes and baritone chants?"

"*Maroon* robes, but yes, deep chants. May I tell Rinpoche you will meet with him?"

I can't exactly start turning down work, but I can't shake the feeling they've got the wrong idea somehow. "Ah, again, I wouldn't want to waste anyone's time." Including my own. "Can you give me a clue about what your teacher hopes I can do for him?" Best guess: one of the monks has been helping himself to the donation jar.

"He prefers to speak with you about it in person."

"Understood. It's just that I only handle certain kinds of cases."

"Okay, so . . . this is about helping him find someone. Call it a missing persons case."

"Someone?"

"A monk. A former student of Jigme Rinpoche."

"He wander off and get lost in Manhattan? That sounds like a job for the police. I'm not a police detective. You know that, right?"

"Yes!" He says the word so emphatically, I wonder if he's getting indignant with me. I've run into this with Chinese clients who thought I was talking down to them just because their English was rough. His is pretty polished. "Mr. Landry, there is more to the situation. You must meet with Rinpoche to understand, okay?"

"Sure."

He asks if four o'clock works for me. I smooth out the calendar page and find my court mandated anger management meeting scrawled in the box for four-thirty. I ask if he can make it sooner or later than that, and we settle on sooner. Norbu gives me the address for the dharma center and tells me to leave my shoes at the door.

"Your office is in Chinatown, yes?" he asks as we wrap up the call.

"That's right."

"So you have followed the news about the recent murders?"

"I'm as familiar as anyone who reads the paper."

"Good, good. I will tell Rinpoche to expect you at three."

I pick the cradle out of the broken particle board and hang up the phone. I had a bad feeling about today, but it turns out Sophie wasn't the worst of it. This guy wants to get me involved with the Chinatown Monster.

2

The first murder happened on New Year's Eve—Gregorian calendar, not Chinese. The police wrote it off as gang violence, but even they knew it was too grisly for gangs. At least that was the word around the deli counters and bars of Little Italy. In Chinatown, nobody talks about the gangs. Certainly not with white guys who smell like pork. The underground gambling parlors in my neighborhood are all run by rival Chinese gangs overseen by the tongs, semi-legitimate Benevolent Associations. Above these groups are the international triads, organized crime syndicates that rival the Italian mafia with deep roots in Chinese secret societies and Southeast Asian drug cartels.

What any of that has to do with Tibetan monks is anybody's guess. Most of my clients are Caucasian. I don't know much about Asia, despite my business address, but I'm old enough to remember when Tibet still looked like a separate country on the Rand McNally globe, and I'm pretty sure the only white powder they have there is snow. The Dalai Lama and his followers seem pretty far removed from the Ghost Shadows gang that runs my street, even if the Diamond Path Dharma Center is only fifteen minutes away on the R train.

I consider cleaning up the mess Sophie Cheung made of my office, but time is tight. Most of it can wait until later, but I crouch and gently pick the little spider plant out of the pottery shards on the floor. I transfer it to a Styrofoam coffee cup, gather as much dirt as I can from the carpet, and pack it in around the roots. It's a cutting from a plant that belonged to Tracy, my late fiancée. I don't have a stellar track record when it comes to things that depend on me surviving, but today will not be the day I lose this plant.

With that tended to, I lock the newly developed photos in the safe with my gun just in case Sophie decides to come back and kick the door down while I'm out. If I can't wear shoes into a Buddhist temple, I'm pretty sure I can't wear a piece either. I slip a fresh notepad into my jacket pocket, lock up, and hit the street where the parade crowd is still milling around among the street vendors. Half a block down Mott, a string of firecrackers goes off. I duck at the sound and turn my back to the bricks, adrenaline spiking and heart thundering before my brain can tell my body it's not artillery. I'm in New York, not *El Chorrillo*.

Nostrils flaring, I regain my composure and hoof it a few blocks to the Canal Street station. I grab a couple of *jiao tze* dumplings from my favorite steam cart on the way, skip the sauce to keep my shirt clean, and tuck into the shredded pork and cabbage snacks on the subway platform while I wait.

I'm still hungry when I step onto the R and rumble uptown to Union Square.

The dharma center looks like any other brick and glass building in the Flatiron District and I almost walk past it, scanning West 14th for numbers. I guess I'm

9

looking for something exotic on the outside, but if not for the name etched above an interwoven diamond-shaped knot on the green glass door it could just as easily be the offices of some college administrators.

The interior is another story altogether. The vestibule is a clean, cream-colored space with a tile floor. Tracks of pin spots on the high ceiling lend it an art gallery or museum vibe, reinforced by the glass display cases lining the walls. But that's where any resemblance to academic Manhattan ends. The content of those cases, the artwork on display, is an assault on the senses so rich in color and detail that it leaves gaudy in the dust on the way to psychedelic grandeur.

Columns of layered silk swatches like neckties in patterns of red, gold, and blue hang from the ceiling, absorbing the echoes of my footsteps as I approach the shoe rack. I step out of my loafers and place them among the others. Gold statues of buddhas, gods, and demons sit atop lotus flowers or dance in rings of fire in the display cases, their serene and fierce faces painted with exquisite detail. On the walls, the pantheon continues: paintings of similar figures floating over paradisiacal landscapes, haloed with gilded rays of light, sitting amid flower blossoms and swirling clouds, each mounted on a four-foot high panel of silk brocade.

Incense smoke spices the air, dark and woody. The lobby is vacant, despite the presence of several pairs of scuffed shoes on the rack. As I pad across the floor, self-conscious about the sorry state of my socks, a short, broad young man with dark skin and a bushy crew cut steps through a curtained doorway behind the reception desk. His sleeveless, mustard-colored shirt is draped with a maroon robe over one shoulder. A string of dark wooden beads twined around his wrist clatters softly as he walks toward me and extends his hand with a smile.

I give the hand a curt shake and do my best to dial down my grip. Everything about the guy makes me want to soften my rough edges.

"Mr. Landry," he says in a soothing tone, and I recognize his voice from the phone call.

"Mr. Norbu?"

The monk nods, still smiling. "Norbu is my first name. Or you may call me by my title, *Geshe*. This way, please. Jigme Rinpoche is expecting you in the shrine room. You will refer to him by his title: *Rinpoche*."

He leads me down a hallway decorated with more sacred artwork. I glimpse a couple of offices and what looks like a library. At the end of the hall, we turn a corner and arrive at another curtain, this one embroidered with the same interlaced diamond knot I saw on the front door.

Norbu draws the curtain aside and waves me into a large hall with more statues and banners. The centerpiece of the shrine is a large golden Buddha seated in lotus position with a begging bowl in his folded hands. After the procession of multi-armed deities with their elaborate crowns and ornaments, he looks about as plain and humble as a golden statue can, situated between pillars emblazoned with turquoise and lapis clouds.

I've seen a lot of Buddhas around Chinatown; most are fat and laughing. This one, fit and trim, radiates an austere serenity.

The smell of incense is stronger here. It hangs in dense layers illuminated by shafts of faint February sunlight filtered through the high windows. A row of wavering flames in silver bowls lines the altar alongside identical bowls of water and rice.

The wood floor is bare except for two meditation cushions. An elderly monk occupies one, his body swaying slightly, eyes almost closed, the syllables of a whispered mantra passing between his lips as beads pass between his fingers. He wears the same maroon and yellow robes as the junior monk, his head dusted with salt-and-pepper stubble. I can't quite place his age—the flesh sags from the arm holding the string of beads, but his fingers are nimble.

Geshe Norbu places a hand at the center of my back and gestures for me to sit. I settle on the empty cushion feeling like I'm disturbing the old man's practice, even though he summoned me. Surely he hears us, but he continues his prayers without looking up.

I let my gaze wander. The paintings in this room are concealed behind red and gold curtains, except for one on the south wall that I can't quite make out. Something monstrous. A dark, horned beast. On a low wooden table beneath the painting, a set of offerings has been arranged. Unlike the clear water and white rice at the foot of the big Buddha statue, here we have a dish of sliced red meat and I swear that's a bottle of Jim Beam.

Well, the Catholics have their bread and wine.

A tassel dangling from the prayer beads passes between the old monk's fingers, his whispering ceases and his eyes flick open, fixed on mine. He smiles, as if we're both in on some private joke.

Norbu speaks up from behind me. "Rinpoche, this is Detective Landry, the private eye you requested."

Jigme Rinpoche nods. In my peripheral vision I detect Norbu bowing and retreating from the room. The senior monk coils the string of beads around his wrist and extends his hand. I offer mine to shake, but he takes it in a gentle squeeze instead.

"I understand you're trying to find someone," I say. "How can I help?"

"Norbu has told you I am seeking a former student. That is true, but requires explanation. For this job, you will need an open mind."

There are little pauses in his speech as he formulates the English.

"I try to keep one on *every* job until it's finished. Investigators have to."

"Do you hold religious views?" he asks.

"No, sir. That's part of my keeping an open mind."

He nods slowly, but doesn't seem displeased with my answer.

"So . . . no strong ideas about afterlife?"

I shake my head. Since Tracy was killed, there have been many times when I wished I had some kind of faith in a world beyond this one. But wishing is for fools.

"The student I am seeking died in 1961."

He gives me a second to react to this. I don't.

Norbu returns and places a silver tray on a low table beside us. He pours two cups of steaming, milky tea and offers one to me. I try a sip. Spicy sweet Indian chai. I'm usually a black coffee guy, but it's good.

"Why do I get the feeling you're not asking me to find his bones or solve a cold case?"

The old monk laughs and says something to his attendant in Tibetan. Norbu nods in agreement and the old man decides to let me in on the joke. "I told Geshe we found the right man for the job."

"On the phone he mentioned the Chinatown murders. Why don't you fill me in? From the beginning."

The Rinpoche sits up straighter and takes a breath. His tone of voice is a touch more formal when he speaks again, as if he's slipped into teaching mode. "Beginning is always difficult to find. All phenomena have many causes and conditions at the root. To know all of the causes and conditions, the karmic seeds that produce the fruit, is to be a Buddha. The man I am seeking—if he *is* a man—I have karma with. I was one of his teachers in his last life."

He gives me another chance to object. I drink my tea. I'll look for the tooth fairy as long as the checks clear.

Jigme Rinpoche slips the coil of beads off his wrist and hands them to me in a pile. The beads clatter into my cupped hand; cold, despite their recent use. "This *mala* belonged to him," Jigme says. "I am purifying it."

I give the string of beads what I hope is enough consideration to satisfy the old man, then hand it back.

"You say he died in 1961. So it wasn't a previous life for *you* when you were his teacher. Forgive me, but you don't look thirty. How old are you, if you don't mind my asking?"

"Seventy-two. I was . . . in my forties when I knew Dorje Tsering. I was not his main teacher, but I gave him tantric initiation. I am responsible for him."

I've only seen the word 'tantra' in magazines

promising interesting sex positions. Rinpoche says something else in Tibetan, and Norbu speaks up: "He says this is difficult to explain. He wants me to translate."

I shift on my cushion to face Norbu while Rinpoche loads him up.

"There are several paths to enlightenment. One path used by Tibetan Buddhists is the *Vajrayana*, the diamond path, what is called tantra. This set of meditations and rituals channel the strong energies of the body for an accelerated path to realization. The practices are safeguarded with initiation and must only be engaged under the supervision of a qualified master. There are dangers. Rather than using meditation techniques as antidotes for emotions such as anger and lust, the raw energy of these states is refined and focused through visualization and mantra. This refined energy is like . . . rocket fuel to propel the practitioner's consciousness to enlightenment in a single lifetime. The poisons become medicines that clarify the mind. Does this make sense?"

I shrug. "Honestly, not much."

Rinpoche continues through the translator.

"When Buddhism came from India to Tibet, many local demons were tamed by masters such as Guru Padmasambhava. They were brought into the service of the dharma as guardians and protectors. Today, many monasteries have a patron protector deity. Wrathful emanations of Buddhas that also have a peaceful manifestation. Meditation on the wrathful form is a powerful way to burn away obstacles to spiritual practice. To obtain the full benefits, the practitioner must identify with the *yidam*, the meditation deity. He must visualize himself as the deity until he feels that he has *become* the deity. This identification can be dangerous—even when cultivating a purely compassionate emanation, such as Avalokiteshvara. In the case of a *wrathful* emanation, the practice must be handled with extreme care. When Jigme Rinpoche initiated Dorje Tsering into the practice, it was an urgent time for our culture. The monasteries were under attack from the Chinese invaders. The traditional structure for such practices was in jeopardy.

"Dorje Tsering over-identified with his wrathful deity. Then his guru, Lama Thubten, was murdered by the Chinese. This, and the slaying of his family members, may have intensified his anger and polluted his consciousness with a desire for vengeance. He gave up his robes and relinquished his vows at a delicate time in his practice. He joined the fight against the Chinese. We believe he was killed by the People's Liberation Army in the Markham district in the spring of 1961. And we fear that he has reincarnated in this life as a powerful emanation of his wrathful meditation deity. Yamantaka, Lord of Death. We fear he has returned with a vendetta."

"You think he's the Chinatown Monster."

Jigme Rinpoche nods. "Yes."

"The police say that's gang violence."

"Your office is in Chinatown, Mr. Landry. What do *you* think?"

"I think you're talking to *me* because the cops wouldn't take any of this seriously for even a minute."

Rinpoche smiles and says to Norbu, "He would make a good monk." Then, to me, "Critical thinking and debate are important for study of philosophy. But what do you think? These mutilations . . . A gang did this?"

"I don't know. And I'm sure the cops don't either, but they have to say *something* to the press. I'm sure the Chinatown gangs are capable of some f— . . . Some very bad acts. To me, a gang trying to make a spectacle sounds more likely than a reincarnated demon monk."

"True," Rinpoche says, "if you don't know how to read the signs."

"Signs?"

The old man gets to his feet with minimal assistance from his attendant. I follow, and he leads me to the one uncovered painting above the table of offerings. Norbu takes away the tea tray and places my sitting cushion atop a pile of them. Looks like our interview is wrapping up. I'm still not sure what they expect from me, but I already know I'm taking the gig, if only for a little while. Even if I prove the monk's theory wrong, I still get paid, and there's enough gold and silver in this place to tell me they're good for it. Also, I have to admit I'm a little intrigued by what they believe. I was raised loosely Catholic, but heaven and hell never really washed with me. Not that I'm likely to buy into the recycling of souls theory, either. But like an alluring song on the radio, I'd like to hear a few more bars before I tune it out.

Rinpoche waves his upturned palm toward the painting, as if pointing at it might anger the deity depicted on the canvas. The pooling cloud of incense stirs in slow eddies. "Yamantaka," he says. "Destroyer of Death."

Against a black background with liquid gold

accents, a blue-black potbellied figure radiating a fan of arms and legs dances on a pile of human and animal corpses in a ring of fire. His head is that of an ox with long, sharp horns ascending from a crown of skulls. Three eyes blaze in a triangle formation above flared nostrils and bared fangs. The creature's hair, beard, and eyebrows are all formed of golden flames. He's naked, except for a necklace and girdle of human heads, his erect penis red-tipped and pointing skyward. His myriad hands and feet are tipped with white claws, each hand clutching a different object: a lion's pelt, a noose, and every variety of weapon—knives, spears, arrows, and throwing stars—all radiating outward in a fan of blades, except for the two hands that meet at the center of the body. Of these, one holds a crescent-shaped knife with an ornamented handle, the other a skullcap splashing blood. The creature's expression is fierce, but a set of additional heads rise in a column above the mane of flaming hair, like a totem pole. The topmost of these is the serene, smiling face of a Buddha.

"You mind if I take a picture?"

Rinpoche nods and I fish my trusty Olympus out of my jacket pocket.

"What does that mean, *Destroyer of Death?*" I ask.

Norbu confers with his teacher in Tibetan, and then explains, "Yamantaka symbolizes cutting through attachment. In his truest form, he represents severing the mind from all bonds. For the one who accomplishes this, there is no rebirth, and therefore, no more death."

"Looks awfully bloodthirsty."

"He is the wrathful manifestation of Manjushri,

buddha of wisdom," Jigme Rinpoche says. "In this form, he is a dharma protector, a guardian of the teachings. But he is not meant to walk the earth, to wield his weapons on city streets."

"If I buy your theory for a minute . . . why here? Why not reincarnate in Beijing and go after Chinese officials?"

Rinpoche claps me on the back and smiles. "Maybe you will help us find out," he says.

I scoff. "Honestly, I don't know where to begin. I mean, what do you expect me to do? Interview doctors and nurses who worked on the maternity wards in the early 60s? Ask them if they remember anyone giving birth to a flaming blue ox?"

Rinpoche shakes his head, annoyed by my thickness, as if all of this should be obvious to me. "You must look into these murders," he says. "See where they lead you. That is all I ask. Will you take the job?"

I feign reluctance. "I have a few contacts on the police force and at the newspapers. I'll dig around a little. No promises, but I'll see what turns up." I bid Jigme Rinpoche farewell with a nod that borders on a bow, and let his attendant escort me out. Following Norbu down the hall, I flip my pad open and ask him to spell some terms for me. Back in the lobby, he hovers over me while I sit on the bench and pull on my shoes. I look up at him, hands on knees, and ask, "What makes him so sure the murders are connected to Tibet?"

Norbu steps behind the reception desk, opens a drawer and roots around in it. At my approach, he sets a folded tabloid on the desktop and glances around the lobby furtively before opening it to a dog-eared page. The blocky headline proclaims DOYERS STREET

SLAUGHTER over a lo-fi newsprint photo in garish colors. The blood looks like cherry syrup, but the photographer soaked up a lot of it, probably from a fire escape with a telephoto lens before the cops covered up the dismembered body. It's hard to extract details from the halftone dots, but I'm pretty sure I see bones jutting out of raw meat on the pavement.

"This photo came to Rinpoche's attention after the second murder," Norbu says. "Combined with reports of the first murder, it is clear the victims were butchered. Carved in the same way that dismemberment of corpses is performed by the *rogyapas* in Tibet."

I raise an eyebrow.

"These are men who carve corpses for feeding to the vultures so that nothing is wasted in the cycle of life."

"You've got to be kidding me."

Across the desk, Norbu has been watching me study the picture. Now he grins. Is he getting off on creeping me out? I meet his gaze and he shrugs. "The ground is too rocky for burial in the mountains. Westerners may find the practice barbaric, but sky burial is a final act of generosity."

"To who?"

"We believe it is better to feed carrion birds than to let the body rot in a box just to deny the worms for a few years. This is a kindness, yes?"

I don't answer him. My pork dumplings are getting restless.

"Dorje Tsering, whose incarnation we seek, was the son of a *rogyapa*—a corpse butcher. As a young man, before taking the monastic vows, he learned the family trade."

20

3

I *meet Sgt.* Joe Navarro at our favorite watering hole later that night. Joe and I served together in Panama. We were thick as thieves with two other grunts in our battalion: Steve Griebling and Larry Yang. Operation Just Cause. General Powell loved the name because even our worst critics would have to say the words. Of course, it didn't take long for those of us who'd been there to put a different spin on it. *Why did we invade Panama? Just 'cause we fuckin felt like it.* Steve was among the twenty-three who didn't come home. Larry and I opened the agency in Chinatown together, and Joe became a cop in the Fifth Precinct.

The place is quiet, like usual. That's what Joe likes about it—he never has to break up a pair of assholes trying to tango while he's off duty. Two guys and a girl are shooting pool on red felt and a couple of regulars are watching the Rangers on TV when I pull up next to Joe at the bar. I order a couple of beers and shots even though he's hardly touched the beer in front of him.

I squeeze his shoulder and ask after his wife and boy.

"They're good, they're good. How about you?"

"Hangin' in there." Joe was there for me when

Tracy died. I don't lie to him that things ever got better again after that, but it's been a while now and I don't harp on it.

He looks me over. "You should get something to eat, man. You're a bag of bones. You need a girlfriend, so's somebody thinks of feeding you once in a while."

Somebody to water me like a plant. I let it slide, knowing he means well. After all, it's been over a year since the accident.

I set my hat down on the bar and he looks at it with a wistful grin. It belonged to Larry, who liked old movies and wanted Insight Detective Agency to have some of that old school style. Larry could wear that hat in earnest. I wear it ironically, but I've made enough of a habit out of it that I sometimes forget it's on my head. I should've left it at the office.

"Long time no see," Joe says. I don't know if he's talking about me or Larry, who shocked us all by eating his gun six months ago.

"You ever run into Amy anymore?" he asks, still looking at the hat.

I scratch the back of my head. "Yeah, I stopped in for eggnog on Christmas Eve. I try to bring her a check now and then if I can slip it into a holiday card."

"Really? You do that?"

"Well it was him that came up with the name and the logo. Got us up and running with a loan from his old man."

Joe squints at me. "No, I mean . . . I'm sure you're good at what you do, Miles, but you can afford that?"

I scoff. "No."

He laughs and we toss back our shots. On to the business at hand.

"So what'd you want to ask me about?"

"The Chinatown Monster."

Joe winces, and not at the bourbon. "Who's your client, the *Daily News*?"

"Hey, now. Would I do that to you?"

"Well then who?"

I shift in my seat and drink my beer. "I'm still getting a feel for this case. It's in that delicate state where I should keep the client's confidence. You cool with that?"

Joe is looking at me differently. I see now that, in spite of the backslapping joviality, he's still a cop first, and all has not been forgiven. "Time will tell," he says. "If a third murder happens and I find out you knew something that could've helped solve the case . . . "

"Nah, it ain't like that. These guys . . . no. They don't know shit. You could almost call my client's interest academic."

Joe's eyebrow jumps and I hurry to add, "Not in a public way. Nobody's writing a book."

"I'll play along for now," he says, "but I'm trusting you, Miles."

I nod and trace a circle in the air over our empty shot glasses for the bartender.

"What do you want to know?"

"For starters, your honest opinion: Do you believe the killer is a gangbanger?"

"The first victim was a known member of the Ghost Shadows." It doesn't get past me that that's not a direct answer.

"But the second wasn't."

Joe continues like I haven't interrupted, "—and whoever killed him wanted to make an impression.

And don't assume the same killer did both murders just because the M.O. matches. You watch TV; you know that could make the second one a copycat."

"Do *you* think the second one is a copycat?"

Joe sips his beer. "Probably not. But that doesn't mean it's not another gang hit."

"On an old street vendor? An ABC? Seems like a stretch." Gang violence is more prevalent among the younger generation, what we call FOBs or Fresh Off the Boat. American Born Chinese tend to steer clear of it. "I know gangsters pressure *shop owners* for protection money, but a street vendor? Even if the old guy defaulted on a loan, why rub him out in such spectacular fashion? Dead is example enough. They don't need the community hating them, right? This was savage butchery. Ain't like the vendor was a rival gang leader. So what's your theory?"

"Who says I have one? Look, everybody in your neighborhood has some connection to gang members. Somebody cared about the old man. That somebody crossed somebody. That's all it takes."

I make a non-committal grunt. "You've ruled out a serial killer?"

"I haven't ruled out anything. Trust me, there's a gang connection. We just haven't found it yet. And if you start talking about serial killers to the press, your sleuthing days in this city are over."

"I told you I'm not working for a reporter. And I get it: If it's a gang thing, it's a Chinatown problem. No mass hysteria."

"That's right. My uncle worked Son of Sam. I don't need *that* kinda circus. That word you used, *academic*, smells like newsprint."

"If it eases your mind, it's a missing persons case, probably unrelated. I'm basically humoring a guy for a couple of legwork payments. Anyway, I get the feeling I'm looking for someone who doesn't exist. Feel better?"

"A little."

"What can you tell me about method?"

Joe flexes his shoulder blades, pops his bad back. "The papers called them mutilations, right? Cops and reporters both like that word. It's vague but provocative. Fact is they were dismemberments."

"Anything ritualistic about the crime scenes?"

"Jesus. You *do* know more than you're telling me."

I stare at him.

Joe sighs, rubs his temple. "This better be a two-way street, Miles."

Now it's my turn to squirm a little. I've been making an effort to sand the rough edges off of my life by sticking to insurance fraud and divorce cases. But Joe is up against a drug epidemic and more than half of the crack and heroin in America passes through my neighborhood. China Cat—Mott Street's hot summer flavor—is so pure the paramedics can't keep up. Joe knows who to call when he needs to employ some non-regulation persuasion, or when a brother cop needs to dispose of a pop-and-drop handgun that may have been used to cut some of the red tape out of the judicial process. I trace a drop of water in a circle on the polished bar. "You know it is," I say.

"There was some foreign matter left in the wounds. Ash that the crime lab says is from incense, and some mineral fragments."

"Mineral fragments?"

"Quartz crystal shards."

"What kind of weapon was used?"

"That we don't know. Blades are hard to pin down. Much harder than bullets. But the crystal shards make us think more than one blade was used. One might have been a sharpened piece of quartz, but the whole job couldn't have been done with a knife like that."

"Why not?"

"Dismembered, remember? You'd need a good strong piece of steel for that. I think we're looking for a professional butcher with gang ties. *That's* my theory. Between you and me."

"But what about the incense?"

"Read up on your Chinese triads. They have initiation rituals. They drink blood mixed with wine and swear oaths from calligraphy scrolls. Gangs and cults have a lot in common."

"Fair enough. You have any witnesses?"

Joe shakes his head and tosses back a handful of bar peanuts, washes them down with beer. I can tell I got all I'm gonna get out of him. "How's anger management going?" he asks.

"Two sessions to go and I haven't slugged the counselor. Yet."

I've used up all my favors with Sgt. Navarro and he's reminding me of it with a nod to the assault charge he vouched for me on back in November, sparing me jail time and the loss of my PI license. Joe lets me chew on that for a minute, then motions for me to pass my flip pad and pen over to him while he downs a shot. He scribbles something and slides the pad back to me: A barely legible name and a pair of streets.

"Who's Sammy Fong?"

"We don't know if that's his real name. He's a FOB, no legal ID. But what's the diff? Everybody changes their name when they get here, anyway. On the books, he's a dish dog at Mappow's, but he's not pulling enough shifts there to support himself. Just enough to make connections with bangers who drop in for tiger meals." He's referring to the free meals gangsters pick up at local restaurants when they aren't delivering a mandarin tree in return for a heavy cash donation. "We've tailed him and confirmed that his real income is stitched together from a variety of Ghost Shadows activities. Not sure if he's been initiated yet or if he's still trying to prove himself. Anyway, he flagged down a cruiser when he found the first victim, a confirmed *dai lo.*"

"David Yu."

"Right. Sammy comes stumbling out of the alley where the body is and sees a police car. Nearly shits himself, but has enough sense to know what running would look like. And this was before he realized how many pieces Yu was in."

"Nobody thinks he did it?"

Joe smiles like he's bitten into something sour. "We didn't rule him out right away, not until he had a tight alibi for the second homicide, but we didn't like him for it, either. He didn't have enough blood on him and he definitely didn't have the level of psychotic cool you would need for the job."

"What's the intersection? His address?"

"It's the street corner where he hangs out the most. Or you might find him at the restaurant. I'm not sure if he still works there. I'm only giving him to you because we've already squeezed him dry. I doubt you'll get anything new, but you *will* let me know if you do."

I nod. "Besides the body, he didn't see anything?"

"It's Chinatown." Joe touches his big, thick-fingered hands to his eyes, ears, and lips, like the three monkeys.

4

In the morning, I drag my broken desk down the stairs to the curb before meeting a client at a coffee shop. I tell her what she'll see in the photos I took of her husband, if she wants to look at them. She only asks to see the one that shows his face the best so she can't kid herself that it isn't him. I am relieved by this show of good sense. Denial is probably the biggest cause of contested invoices in my line of work, but I also don't need her crying all over the prints in the coffee shop where we conduct our business.

With that done, I make a few inquiries among the neighborhood kids I've cultivated as informants. Whenever I have a few bucks to spare, I toss a *Spider Man* comic or a *Playboy* their way and get a good return on investment. Today, I ask them about Sammy Fong. They don't know much except that he found the chopped up body of a *dai lo*, a gang big brother, and they want to tell me all about it in gory detail until I tell them I already know about that, like everybody else in New York, and then they want *me* to tell *them* all the gory details that weren't in the paper.

I promise the little pack of dogs a paper bag full of hard liquor nips if they can get me something substantial on the guy's business without dropping my name. I have very little faith that any of them grasp the concept of discretion, but they're all I've got and they eagerly accept, so I send them off to do my bidding. Watching them go, I feel a little like Mickey setting the brooms loose to do his dirty work in *Fantasia*.

It rained hard the day before Chinese New Year, but it's colder today. You can almost taste the threat of snow.

Knowing it will take my urchins a few hours to gather intel, I head up to the main branch of the N.Y. Public Library—scarfing down a sandwich at a deli near the *Times* building before wading into the stacks, where food will be forbidden—to read up on Tibetan Buddhism and see if yesterday's crash course checks out with published sources.

The Deuce, 42nd Street, exerts a gravitational tug on my lower nature, and the animal in me almost takes a detour down Grindhouse Row toward the flashing bulbs and XXX posters. I keep my eye on the paycheck and stay my course to 5th Avenue, passing the Armed Forces recruiting station on the corner of 7th, where I don't have to sidle through a crowd of volunteers lined up to defend Kuwait. Operation Desert Shield became Desert Storm when Bush's January 15th ultimatum passed last month. It might not be a ground war yet, but everybody can hear the drums and nobody's in a hurry to kill or die for the price at the pump. I spare a thought for old friends still enlisted, and then I'm jogging up the white steps, striding between the lion statues that flank the NYPL entrance, and reading the words I always look for engraved in the granite, part of the ritual of research:

BUT ABOVE ALL THINGS
TRUTH
BEARETH AWAY
THE VICTORY

Not a bad mantra for a private eye.

Two hours of combing through indexes and reading pages out of context later, my head is heavy and my eyes are sluggish. I've never been a big reader and this is not light fare. I've skipped over Buddhism 101 with this case and gone straight to the hardcore esoteric stuff. The 14th Dalai Lama's popular book on tantra confirms the basic philosophy, but to check the details on Yamantaka, I've had to sift through tomes written by western academics. I'm not surprised that the fellows writing in their native English are less clear than the Tibetan master, but I try not to wade in too deep, keeping my focus on checking the books against my notepad. What the two monks told me yesterday checks out. Their explanation of tantra was truthful, if a little oversimplified.

I squeeze my eyes shut and rub my temples. I need coffee, and by now the kids might have something for me, so I head back down to Chinatown, taking a detour into The Magickal Childe bookshop on West 33rd on the way. Of the stack of books I've spent my morning with at the library, the one title I'm fascinated by is the infamous *Tibetan Book of the Dead,* and now I want a copy I can mark up. The shop is a cramped little hole in the wall that reeks of voodoo oils and herbs. Ceremonial swords and shelves of dusty glass jars cover the walls. A leather-bound copy of the *Necronomicon* takes pride of place in the display window and again at the cash register, where an old warlock is painting his nails black. I read enough Lovecraft in high school to know it's a hoax, but I manage to find a paperback edition of the more authentic guide to the underworld in the Eastern section and leave the shop with it in a brown paper bag. Weird energy in that joint. I only know the place because of a cheating husband who was banging a witch.

I crack the book open on the subway and read the introduction. Grimy tiled stations flash past as we rumble through the tunnel, but I hardly spare them a glance and nearly miss my stop, lost in the cosmology.

Aboveground, I pick up a second paper bag, this one a sack of nips from a liquor store. I feel a pang of guilt buying alcohol for sixth graders, but they're gonna get it somewhere.

Kenny, the pudgy leader of the little pack of scrappers, is waiting for me on the steps to my office. The kid looks tough enough with his spiky frosted hair, tight black jeans, and throwing star necklace, but he's all boy when he cracks a smile at the two paper bags in my hands. Greedy little bastard probably thinks I bought too many bottles to fit in one. My return grin feels rueful on my face. Kenny will probably be in the Ghost Shadows or the Dragons within four years, dead within ten. He's already working on the uniform. All he needs to finish it off is a pair of white Keds, a satin jacket with a dragon embroidered on the back, and a beeper.

"Whaddaya got for me?" I ask, as I sit down beside him on the steps.

He holds out his open hand.

I slap one of the bags into it and watch him feel the shape through the paper. He pokes his nose into it and says, "A *book?* What the hell?" Kenny speaks better English than most of his elders who alternate between Hong Kong Cantonese and fragments of it.

"Relax," I say, shaking the other bag so he can hear the chiming of little glass bottles. "The book is mine. You get these after you tell me something I can use."

Kenny tosses the bag with the book onto the step at my feet. "Sammy Fong is a Ghost."

"Wow, what a revelation."

"That's why he was going to meet David Yu that night in the Bloody Angle. He thought Yu was gonna cap him because he was selling black market cigs to kids, but he went to the meeting anyway to talk him out of it, cause if he can't be a Ghost, he might as well be dead anyway, right?"

"Why does a *dai gor* like David Yu care about kids buying cigarettes?"

"Because he's not getting a cut! Sammy was doing this one thing on the side without telling his big brother about it. Guess he thought if he only sold to a few kids, he wouldn't get caught. But if you want to be a Ghost, the tong gets a piece of everything you do, right? Sammy messed up. But crazy thing is he goes to the alley to meet his *dai gor*, and who comes out alive? Sammy! And David Yu comes out in a bunch of garbage bags. But after he finishes freaking out about the killing and he realizes the cops aren't gonna put it on him, he goes right back to selling cigs. Maybe he thinks nobody knows about his side business now that Yu is dead."

"How do *you* know?"

Kenny laughs. "I buy from him, dipshit."

"Watch it. Does anyone—and I don't mean kids, but the adults you hear talking—do *they* think Sammy killed David Yu?"

Kenny fidgets because he knows his story points in that direction, but no, no one does. No one who knows the streets, anyway. Sammy Fong's continued existence is proof of that. The kid casts his gaze at the pavement while telling me what he knows is the childish sounding part, but after the little bit of gang intel, it's all he has left: "People say it was a monster that got David Yu in the Bloody Angle. Like a demon or a dragon man or something. It's bullshit, right?"

His eyes dart up and meet mine. He's heard this from adults and wants one to refute it. As if the monsters he lives among and aspires to become aren't bad enough.

"Don't believe everything you hear in the tea parlors and laundromats." I hand him his paper bag and resist the impulse to muss up his spiky hair. "But keep your ears open for me, bud."

"You bet. See ya."

Kenny trots off with his loot, the other boys clamoring around him. I go upstairs and transfer the book to my shoulder bag with my compact camera and note pad, thinking that I might play the angle of a reporter when I find Sammy. It could easily backfire, but if he thinks there's an opportunity to send a signal that could improve his standing or cover his ass with the tong, he just might talk to me. I'll need to get a read on him before committing to it.

I hesitate at the door, then slip out of my jacket to strap on the shoulder holster with the Colt 1911 before slipping back into it and heading out.

+ —— + —— +

They call Doyers Street Murder Alley. It's the perfect place for any killing you would want to commit under the cover of gang violence. One block long with a sharp ninety-degree angle in the middle, it runs from Pell Street to the Bowery at Chatham Square and is—according to the cops—the bloodiest intersection in America. There are probably two reasons for this. One is the sharp bend in the street whence comes the nickname, "The Bloody Angle," a feature that lends itself well to gang ambushes. The other is a pedestrian tunnel that runs under the buildings, offering quick escape routes to East Broadway and Catherine.

A tight channel, like a slaughterhouse chute, seldom traveled by cars, it's a street that seems to serve no purpose as there are plenty of other ways to get where you're going without it. Which is not to say it's devoid of cultural heritage. Home to the oldest Chinese tea house in America, the Nom Wah, and the site of the 1905 Chinese Theater Massacre in which Hip Sing gunmen opened fire on a group of On Leong gangsters under cover of a string of firecrackers, today the street bustles with knick-knack shops, barbers, and restaurants between graffiti stricken corrugated metal panels at street level and rat-infested tinderbox tenements above.

The once secret tunnel has been converted into an underground shopping arcade where, on December 27 at 2:17 A.M., Sammy Fong found the remains of David Yu in a pool of blood long after the retailers, acupuncturists, and fortune tellers brave enough to hang a shingle down there had locked up for the night.

But I don't find Sammy in Murder Alley today. I find him right where Joe Navarro told me I would: smoking a (probably untaxed) cigarette in another alley, a garbage-reeking space piled with empty wooden vegetable crates behind the kitchen of Mappow's restaurant. He's lanky but not without some muscle, dressed in black jeans and a white sleeveless t-shirt, arms and pockmarked face glazed with sweat from the kitchen steam, a white bandanna tied under his shaggy hair. He reminds me of an extra in a karate movie, but I've had enough karate for one week.

Spur of the moment I decide to forgo the reporter angle and play it straight with him. "Sammy," I say, as I come around the corner from where I've been watching him. I'm not even sure this is the kid I'm looking for—they've kept his photo out of the papers— but he looks up at the sound of his name and the fear on his face confirms it.

He tosses the butt at the ground and backs up toward the screen door to the kitchen. I can see woks and colanders hanging on the wall, hear voices calling over the sizzle of stir-fry, but there's no one in sight of the back door. "What do you want?" he asks and sniffles. I don't know what he looks like on a good day, but he doesn't look well to me today. It's the look of a man who has not been getting much sleep. And no jacket or even sleeves in February? I'm sure it's hot in that kitchen over the dishwashing sink, but it's in the thirties out here.

I flip open my wallet and show him my PI license. "Miles Landry. I'd like to talk to you about the night that made you famous."

"You a cop?"

"Private eye."

He still looks like a skittish animal contemplating fight or flight, so I say, "Relax, buddy. You ever hear of a tong hiring a white detective?"

He runs the back of his hand under his nose, then opens the screen door and reaches inside. I very conspicuously slide my right hand into my jacket like I'm about to recite the Pledge of Allegiance . . . or draw heat. His hand emerges holding a gray sweatshirt. The pockets don't look heavy. He puts it on, knowing that his cigarette break is going to run longer than usual, but the sweatshirt is a good sign: he's curious enough to at least want to know my deal. He lights another and tries to act tough. "You got until I finish this to tell me who sent you. I'm at work."

"Yeah, keeping up the act of a day job is wise when the cops and mob bosses are watching where your money comes from."

"You working for a newspaper?"

"No."

"Who then?"

"Nobody who can cause you trouble. Nobody who wants to. But *I* can if you don't help me. Did you see who killed David Yu in the tunnel?"

Sammy scoffs at the worn out question. "No." He draws hard on the cigarette, the orange line turning an inch of paper to ash in a breath, telling me time's almost up.

"Let me rephrase that: Did you see, hear, or smell anything unusual before or after you found the remains?" I'm thinking of the traces of incense Joe mentioned.

"No. And I wouldn't tell no fuckin *gwailo* if I did." He tosses the butt at my feet.

37

"You'll tell *this* white devil, my friend, or you'll find yourself in Hell."

He scoffs. "You're not even a cop. Why you think I'm gonna tell you more than I tell them?"

"Because the cops don't know about your black market cigarette racket with the kids."

His face blanches a little at that, but he keeps up the tough facade. "Ooh, you're gonna tell the cops on me. Like they care about that with all the gambling and killing going on. Ain't like I'm slinging horse."

"No, you're just trying to graduate to that." I flash him a nice white predatory smile. "And who said anything about telling the cops? See, what I'm thinking of doing while you finish washing the dishes, is taking a leisurely stroll up Mott Street to that pretty pagoda with the red lanterns. The On Leong Chinese Businessman's Association? Because the gentlemen up in that castle might be *very* interested in learning about your side business. See, those cigs might not be taxed by Governor Cuomo, but they sure as hell would be taxed by the local Chinese king if he knew about 'em. If he knew one of his Ghosts was cutting him out of the action."

Sammy looks cold again, in spite of the sweatshirt.

"I bet when they summoned you after the cops released you, they didn't mention your side racket, so you figured you were in the clear. Your big brother was gonna talk to you about it that night, tell you to drop it before the bosses found out. Only he got butchered first."

"You don't know jack."

"Well, I'll let you get back to work, Sammy. Scrubbing dishes is good thinking work. A man's mind can really ponder things while his hands are busy. I'm gonna go have a coffee across the street and do some thinking of my own, about whether or not to take that walk."

I touch the brim of my hat and, turning to leave, hear him mutter, "*Molla Focka.*"

I settle into a seat facing the door at a corner table in a busy little teahouse. I take out my copy of *The Tibetan Book of the Dead* and try to focus on it while keeping one ear peeled for the chimes tied to the door, wondering how long it will take before Sammy Fong comes in singing a different tune.

They don't have coffee so I settle for tea, hoping it has enough caffeine to help me plough through the rest of the introduction. From what I can glean, the book is unique among religious guides to the afterlife. Meant to be read to a dying person, the prayers in its pages are designed to wake the untethered consciousness up and remind it that the visions it's experiencing of the peaceful and wrathful deities are actually illusions with no inherent existence. If the dying person can recall this lesson, and if he can remember that even his own soul or self is equally empty of absolute reality, then he may attain enlightenment and escape the otherwise endless cycle of birth, death, and suffering.

It's fascinating stuff, but it requires a different level of focus than the horror paperbacks I tend to favor. I find my mind wandering, so I flip through the pages randomly, taking in the poetry and imagery, seeing if anything jumps out at me. The words are getting fuzzy and I have to reread even these fragments to comprehend them. It's too warm in the teahouse, and my head starts to nod.

Animal-headed gods and demons dance on lotus flowers in the sky and drag the wandering soul around by a noose, telling him that he cannot escape the consequences of his karma. I guess this green tea is pretty weak compared to black java. I catch myself dozing and snap to with a start. A glance at my watch tells me that Sammy is one ballsy little fledgling gangbanger who probably isn't gonna show if he hasn't already.

The next thing I know a knockout redhead is leaning over me, shaking my shoulder—her sky-blue eyes are dazzling, even behind glasses. She has my book in her hand, offering it to me. "You dropped this. You don't want a holy book like that touching the floor." She says it with a smile, so it doesn't come across as preachy, but I'm embarrassed just the same.

"Thanks," I tell her, straightening up and taking the book, "but I'm not a Buddhist."

She nods. "Somehow I guessed that."

I sit up and check my tie to make sure I haven't been drooling on it. It's beaded with mist, but my teacup is no longer steaming. I push the cup aside and gesture at the empty seat across from me, offering it to her. "And are you? A Buddhist?"

Her pink mouth does a little twist. "Mmm . . . I'm about seventy-five percent Buddhist on a good day."

I like her already. "What's the other twenty-five?"

"Maybe pagan or agnostic, but, then again, Buddhism might be twenty-five percent pagan and agnostic, too."

"So you have commitment issues. Me too. Can I

buy you a cup of tea for saving my book from the floor?"

"Or saving *you* from bad karma?" she says with a smile.

"Take your pick."

"Okay. But only if you tell me what a cop is doing reading *The Tibetan Book of the Dead*."

"I'm not a cop." I stand up and offer my hand. "Miles Landry, PI, at your service."

She gives it a squeeze. "Gemma Ellison, student, at yours."

Gemma sits and I signal the waitress for another tea. I ask her where she goes to school. Columbia, majoring in Asian Studies. That explains her familiarity with my reading material and why she's the only other Caucasian in a Chinese teahouse in the middle of a weekday.

"So what made you pick up the book?" she asks. "Contemplating mortality?"

I consider telling her I'm just curious about other cultures, but my gut tells me lying isn't the right place to start with her. "I'm trying to help some monks out. Figured I should get a little background."

"That's cool. Are you helping them find a reincarnated master?"

I'm pretty good at not wearing my reactions, but that catches me off guard. I cover with a laugh. "If I told you, I'd have to . . . "

"Yeah, yeah, aren't you quite the cliché?"

"What? You've seen a lot of reincarnation detectives on TV?"

She blows on her hot tea and flashes a thin but genuine smile. "What do you think of it so far?"

"Eh . . . it's not what I expected. Seems more like psychology than religion."

"I agree."

"But it's also mythical. Like a beautiful dream and a terrible nightmare all in one."

"Maybe death is like that."

"Maybe. I'm still on the introduction. I'm sure it'll lose me when I really get into it."

She nods and seems to be considering something, then says, "You could always meet me here for tea if you have questions. It is my field of study, after all."

I have to wonder if our meeting is more than serendipity. Are the monks crafty enough to enlist some pretty young thing to keep tabs on me?

"That's kind of you. I may do just that." I slide a couple of business cards out of my wallet and pass them to her with a pen, ask her to write her number on the back of one and keep the other.

She jots the number down while I watch the street through the window. Still no sign of Sammy. I guess I'm not as intimidating as I try to be.

"I was joking about looking for a reincarnation," she says, "but I am curious about what you're doing for the monks."

"So am I." I put a few bills on the table and slip my book into the bag. Beyond the window, misty rain is gathering, but I'm anxious to check on the dish dog one more time before I head back to the office.

"Are you a security consultant for them?" Gemma asks, gathering her own things.

"Why would monks need security?"

"For His Holiness's visit to New York."

"His Holiness?"

"The Dalai Lama."

"The Dalai Lama is coming to New York City? Funny, they failed to mention that. When?"

"October, I think. He's been invited to perform the Kalachakra initiation at Madison Square Garden."

"Huh."

"You're feeling a little out of your depth, aren't you?" Her tone is sympathetic, so I don't bristle.

I wave the card she wrote on like I'm helping the ink to dry. "I'll be calling you for sure. Just as soon as I know what my questions are."

The mist is thickening to rain when I come around the corner of the kitchen alley again. Rats scavenging around the dumpster brazenly ignore my approach and go on sniffing at rotting vegetables through the broken slats of wooden crates. One of those crates has been moved, cocked askew beneath the fire escape from which Sammy Fong's body dangles at the end of a rope, revolving slowly clockwise and back again. His eyes bulge out of his waxy face, staring at me. A wave of nausea swells in my stomach and I focus on the concrete at my feet until it passes.

I approach the body. The rope could be a piece of laundry line from a nearby tenement. Thin enough to almost cut into the flesh of his neck. If he wasn't such a lightweight, it might have.

There's only one way in and out of the alley—the way I came from—and I'm hit with the strong urge to retreat before I'm seen. The fire escape is far enough away from the kitchen door that the body can't be seen from inside, but it's only a matter of time before someone, probably Sammy's boss, pokes their head out the door looking for him.

There's something tucked under the bandanna he's still wearing—a dash of color, almost concealed by a curtain of sweaty black hair.

I step up onto the crate and pluck it out, knowing that in doing so, I'm making the decision to keep it, to steal and withhold evidence from the scene of a suicide or murder. Joe Navarro's disapproving face surfaces in my mind and I push it aside, driven by the need to know what I'm looking at.

The rain patters down in earnest now. I shelter the delicate object under the brim of my hat, examining it before tucking it into my pocket. Turns out it's not the sort of thing that holds fingerprints.

A peacock feather.

5

BACK AT MY OFFICE, I pour myself a bourbon and set it down on the folding card table I'm using as a temporary desk. I need to slow down and think things through. Maybe it *was* a suicide.

My gut says no.

I check my watch. I took the three blocks back to my office at a brisk walk and I'm not sure of exactly how much time has passed between the hanging and my discovery of the body. I reach for my glass and find myself picking up the phone instead. It's just a hunch. I know it won't prove anything. But before any more time can slip away, I've called the dharma center.

An unfamiliar male voice answers: "*Tashi delek!* Diamond Path Dharma Center. How may I help you?"

"Is Geshe Norbu available?"

"He's out on an errand. Would you like to leave a message?"

I leave my name, then hang up and pull Gemma Ellison's card from my wallet. I turn it over in my fingers and sip my drink, relaxing into the liquid heat and letting the impulse to keep making phone calls until I have some answers fade. One thing I learned in the army is that sometimes, when you're rattled, you have to resist the urge to react. The brain hates uncertainty. It wants to resolve things, even if it means making a situation worse. I need to live with Sammy's death and the fact that I may have caused it, and not go lashing out blindly, or I'll end up calling Joe Navarro and everything will spiral out of control.

As I settle down, I realize my eagerness to call Gemma is motivated partly by a desire to see her again. That she might be able to shed some light on the significance of the feather is just an excuse. There are other resources at my disposal for finding out what a peacock feather represents to different Asian cultures, and, anyway, it's bad practice to trust someone just because they're attractive.

The phone rings. It's Geshe Norbu. The connection sounds thinner than the call I just made to the dharma center.

"Geshe. You got my message? Are you at the dharma center?"

"Ah, I didn't know you called. I'm in the lobby. I was in your neighborhood for some shopping. May I come up, or are you busy with another client?"

"I'll buzz you in. Third floor."

Without a desk drawer to stow it in, I knock back what's left of my drink and put the glass on a shelf before Geshe Norbu shows up at my door. He's carrying a white plastic grocery bag with red Chinese characters on it. I offer him the chair across from the card table. He adjusts his robes and sits.

"So you were in the neighborhood."

"I come here for masala spices and some other things. How is it going?"

"Well, it's only been a day. I'm afraid I don't have anything for you yet."

"Of course. I understand. How did the meeting with your policeman friend go? Did you learn anything?"

I lean forward and click my pen. The table wobbles. "Listen. The way I work is I do the job as I see fit and report back when I have something substantial. I don't usually give my client a play-by-play. It's a waste of time, and things take time to play out."

"Yes. I see. I'm not asking for details. I just wanted to say that if you haven't met with this man yet—"

"I have."

"Did you mention us to him? The dharma center or Rinpoche?"

"No, sir. I don't say who my clients are if I don't have to. But what's your concern? It might be a little embarrassing to *me*, admitting I'm looking for a reincarnated demon, but what do you guys have to worry about? You're monks. Surely you haven't done anything wrong."

Norbu visibly relaxes in the chair. He picks at a fuzz ball where the wool of his robe has pilled. "We Tibetans are refugees, guests in other countries. We have to learn the rules wherever we go. We try to be *good* guests and not cause trouble. Our own government has been in exile since 1959 when His Holiness the Dalai Lama escaped to India, so wherever we go, we are in a difficult political position. This is an important year for spreading awareness of our cause. They are calling 1991 'The Year of Tibet.' We have invited His Holiness to visit New York, to give teachings and initiation. On this trip, he also plans to meet with an American president for the first time at the White House."

I whistle.

"All of this requires permits and visas for a retinue of traveling monks . . . and the goodwill of the people of New York."

I lean back in my chair, clicking my pen, then point it at him with a devilish grin. "You're savvy to the politics of running a religion. The public relations angle."

"The police are part of the city's government. If the Tibetan community hosting the Dalai Lama is believed to have connections to gang violence or murders . . . " He shakes his head solemnly and sucks his teeth. "It could jeopardize everything. You must understand."

"You didn't think to mention this when you hired me to poke around?"

"Rinpoche has higher concerns, but some of us must be practical."

"Seems like it's in your best interest to not stir the pot. Let the police go on thinking these killings are just Chinatown being Chinatown."

"Do they?"

"Hard to say. But they like to keep *their* PR under control, too."

The phone rings. "Don't worry, Geshe. Your interest in the Chinatown Monster is still confidential." I raise a finger and answer the phone. Speak of the devil. It's Sgt. Joe Navarro.

"What the hell did you do, Miles?"

"Scuse me?"

"I give you a name yesterday and today we find the guy swinging on a rope."

"*What?*"

"Did you talk to him?"

"He said he had nothing for me."

"What else? Did you threaten him, lose your temper?"

"No. I kept cool."

"And?"

"I applied a little pressure. I dug up a little side business he was running that could piss off the tong. You know how they're big on non-compete clauses."

"Very funny. What was he into?"

"Just a little slice of black market cigarettes. Probably through an acquaintance in a rival gang. I said I might take a walk up to the pagoda and tip them off about it. I guess he thought his secret died with David Yu."

"You think Sammy butchered David Yu?"

"Hell no." I look at the monk sitting across from me. He's studying his nails. They're a little long, but clean. "Fong is a bit player. *Was* a bit player, you're telling me?"

"Turn on your TV. The media's all over it. It's not my case, thank God, but I never should have talked to you."

"Look, Joe, I don't think he took me serious enough to check out over it. If he was scared, why not give me something?"

"You didn't make good on the threat? Don't even think about lying to me."

"No. Jeez, Joe. It was just a tactic. I never for a minute thought about actually talking to those guys. C'mon, you know what this is. I'm an extra crossing the stage between scenes that have nothing to do with me."

I dig through the piles of paper on the card table,

find the remote, and click on the TV perched on the file cabinet across the room. Geshe Norbu turns to look at it over his shoulder. A young woman in a raincoat holding a microphone boxed with the station call letters fades in standing in front of the alley where I was less than an hour ago. With the sound muted I can't hear what she's saying, just Joe in my ear.

"You had nothing to do with it? What a load of crap. Even if this is the Chinatown Monster taking out Fong because he witnessed the previous kill, you're still the catalyst. You might have been bluffing, but the killer keeping an eye on Sammy Fong doesn't know he won't crack for you."

I don't know what to say to that, so I let him fume out.

Finally, he asks the question worrying him the most. "Did you give Fong your card?"

"No."

A breath of relief distorts in my ear.

"I'm with a client," I say. "Can I call you back?"

"Don't bother. Stay away from this, Miles." And with that, he hangs up.

Norbu has turned his chair to face the TV. "Sorry," I say, and raise the remote to turn it off. But the monk raises his hand to stop me. "That man," he says, pointing to the photo of Sammy Fong. "I've seen him before. He was at the dharma center. He is dead?"

"What did he want with the dharma center?"

"I don't know. Geshe Tenzin confronted him and he went away, but we found him watching the entrance again a week later."

"How long ago was this?"

"Three weeks?"

"You're sure it was him."

"I'm certain."

"Did he threaten anyone or steal anything?"

"No."

I turn the TV off. Norbu is still looking at the blank screen when he says, "He was killed?"

"Might have been suicide."

Turning to face me again, his expression is grave and . . . empathetic?

"He was found hanged," I say. This detail gets no reaction. Norbu would make a decent detective, I think. "There was a noose in the painting of Yamantaka that you and Rinpoche showed me yesterday. And I've been doing a little reading, so I know that souls are dragged around by nooses in *The Tibetan Book of the Dead*."

"You are reading the *Bardo Thodol*?"

"I always do my homework. But you're the expert. Do you think a hanging makes it another kill by the Chinatown Monster? Yamantaka?"

Norbu's head wobbles on his shoulders. "Yamantaka wields many weapons."

I have no other card to play, so I take the peacock feather from where I've tucked it in my shirt pocket and show it to him. His features flicker for a second, a jack-o'-lantern in a breeze. "What does this mean to you?" I ask.

"Where did you find it?"

"My question first. What does it symbolize? Anything?"

He reaches for it and I let him take it. He sniffs it and I wonder why I haven't yet. "Smells like incense," he says. "Peacock feathers are sometimes used in tantric ritual. There is a text called *The Wheel of Sharp Weapons*. A meditation on the destruction of the ego by Yamantaka. The first verses refer to peacocks in a poison grove."

"What do those lines mean?"

"In India it was believed that the vibrant colors of peacock feathers resulted from the birds eating poisonous plants, transforming the poisons into something beautiful. The text was written by the Indian master Dharmaraksita, a yogi who practiced and composed his verses in a jungle, surrounded by predators. The peacock is a symbol of the Bodhisattvas—Buddha warriors who turn away from nirvana on the brink of enlightenment and choose to continue reincarnating in the realms of suffering to help liberate others until the very last sentient being attains enlightenment."

"*That's* what that Steely Dan tune is about?"

"Excuse me?"

"Never mind. Go on."

"*The Wheel of Sharp Weapons* says that peacocks thrive on the essence of virulent poison. Likewise, heroes in the jungle of cyclic existence do not seek the gardens of happiness and prosperity because heroes thrive in the forest of suffering, transforming poison emotions into something beautiful to inspire others."

"What would the killer be trying to tell us by leaving this feather on the trail?"

"Maybe that he sees himself as a hero, a Bodhisattva. Are you sure it was left by the killer?"

I shrug. "Feels right, but that doesn't make the killer a Tibetan. I need to find out if it might have a different meaning to a Chinese gang member."

"I see." Norbu places the feather on the table, leans forward and picks up my pen. He seems to be searching for a blank scrap of paper, so I flip a small legal pad to a clean sheet and pass it to him. He writes, then says, "This is the name of an oracle. Not Tibetan. Chinese, but she is very good. You should see her."

"You want me to get my fortune told?"

"Of course, we will reimburse you."

I've heard of psychics helping the police, but in this case it seems like going from fluffy to flaky. Still, I feel a chill at the thought of talking to a psychic. If there is such a thing as the real deal, could she pass me a message from Tracy? From beyond? As soon as the notion arises in my mind, I recognize it for what it is: the desperate hope that enables charlatans to drain bank accounts. But I can't help how readily it presented itself. Maybe I'm not as much of a skeptic as I'd like to believe. Anyway, these Buddhists would say that my dead fiancé is already in another body.

"I think we should stick with following witness leads and physical evidence."

"But this *is* physical evidence," Norbu says, pointing the pen at the feather on the table. "Mrs. Lao advertises her services as a coin throwing fortune teller. *I Ching*. But many know her as a gifted object reader. Simply by holding this feather, she may be able to tell you something about who it belonged to."

I raise an eyebrow.

"The killer would have been in a strong emotional state when he last touched it. This would leave an imprint that she can read."

"I thought Buddhist masters don't *have* strong emotional states."

He laughs. "Mr. Landry, if he was a master, he wouldn't be a killer."

6

AFTER **N**ORBU **L**EAVES, I lock up the office and climb the stairs to the roof for a smoke. I can't see squat from the top of my building, just graffiti on red brick in every direction with the skyscrapers in the gray drizzly distance, but I still like it up here better than down on the street when I need some nicotine to help me think. The car and truck exhaust is a little thinner up here, and maybe it's my imagination but I think it makes the tobacco taste better.

I stand on the gravely tar paper—not too close to the edge because I have a thing about heights—and by the time I'm on my second smoke, I've almost decided to drop the case. It's getting way too hot and I'm only one day into it. I don't need to piss off Joe and his buddies in blue any more than I already have. But something is niggling at me. I'm trying to figure out how to get at least one payment for legwork out of the monks before I bail, but when I think about telling Jigme Rinpoche that I can't help him, there's this resistance, and it's not just the money.

Is it the allure of their confidence about life after death? The promise of inner peace?

I'm turning it over in my mind, like a man in the

54

dark trying to figure out the shape of something he found in his pocket, when I hear fast footsteps on the gravel behind me. There's not enough time to react before I'm slammed into the low brick wall, watching my cigarette disappear down the chasm on its way to Mott Street. Then: hands around my ankles, gotta be two guys—one on each leg—and I'm kicking at first but maybe that's not such a good idea because a second later those hands are the only things keeping me from plunging to my death. My heart is out of my mouth, following the cigarette down into the traffic, and some detached part of my mind is wondering if I'll hit a street vendor cart, a pedestrian, or just pavement and thinking, *scream on the way down so you don't kill anybody,* but they haven't dropped me, they haven't dropped me, and that's good, that means they want to talk.

I wriggle a little, try to turn my head and get a look at my assailants, but one leg slips through the grip a few inches, so I give up. Somehow my heart that should be splattered like a tomato on the sidewalk for falling out of my mouth is still stampeding in my chest.

"What you want with Sammy Fong, dickhead?" A Chinese accent.

I can't pull enough breath to answer with the fear constricting my lungs. It's like the atmosphere is too thin to squeeze oxygen out of it. I force my way through it and get some words out. "Same as everybody else. Witness. He found David Yu."

"Who hired you?"

I drag air. It's getting easier. Weird how you can get used to hanging out on death's doorstep. The blood is rushing to my head. "Nobody who gives a shit about Chinatown gangs," I say.

The hands on my calves let go and I lurch toward oblivion. They catch me again at my shoes and I'm wishing I was wearing tight-laced boots instead of cheap loafers.

"*Who?* I don't ask a third time."

"Monks. Tibetan monks. They're superstitious. Want to find out if the Chinatown Monster is a demon or some shit. It's good for both of us. I don't even want to know who you are. They pay me to chase shadows and . . . "—wrong word—"Not *Ghost* Shadows, they don't care about gangs, they don't care!"

When I hear his voice again, it's closer. He's leaning over the edge of the building to get close to my ears. No one below is looking up. I want to scream, but I think that would be the last sound I ever make. I'm not doing that unless they drop me. "This monk the same one been sniffing around Chinatown?"

"What?"

"Little fat guy who buys cardamom and ginger?"

Norbu's been making his own inquiries? That's news, but not a surprise. These thugs must have just missed him leaving the building or they wouldn't be asking.

"I . . . " I almost say *I don't know* but I don't think my ticker can take another lurch. "Yeah, that guy. Norbu. He's harmless. I'm telling you, he thinks an ox headed demon is the Chinatown Monster. Let him think that. Let him think it. Worry about the cops, not him or me. I'm just trying to keep the lights on."

For a harrowing moment there's no more talk, just the wind in my ears and the horns below. They haul me up, my belly scraping across the bricks, until I'm dumped on the tarpaper.

I look up at my antagonists, shielding my eyes against the lowering sun pouring through tattered cloud cover on the horizon. It takes a second to register, but I'm looking at a heavyset Caucasian with a bald spot in a blue windbreaker and khakis and a young Chinese guy in a motorcycle jacket and jeans. Benny Chen, ironically one of the only Chinese cops working the Fifth Precinct. I've seen him with Joe on a couple of occasions.

"*Benny?* What the hell? And who's this asshole?"

Benny laughs and nods at the white guy, who hikes his pants up, spits at the gravel, and says, "Detective Grolnic at your service. Lucky thing we caught you and gave you a hand up. Maybe you should take your smoke breaks on the street, Landry."

"You son-of-a-bitch." I'm talking to Chen. He's the one who pumped me for my client's identity in his overwrought gangster voice, the one who almost made me piss my pants, and now my needle swings from fear to rage in a heartbeat. "You son-of-a-bitch." I kick off the ground and blitz into him. He's a lightweight and his feet leave the ground before I slam him into the brick cube that houses the door to the stairwell. Grolnic is yelling at me, maybe he's even drawn his gun, but I could give a rat's ass. What's he gonna do, shoot me? I'm in a red haze, cursing Benny out until he knees me in the jewels and cuts my tirade short.

Grolnic decides to move on me with his big hands rather than pretend his gun has any place in this off-the-books house call. It works. He lays a couple of thrust punches into my floating ribs—I'll have the purple to show for it later—then swings me around and bounces the back of my head off the graffiti-tagged bricks.

I growl at him while he holds me pinned by the collar. "Joe send you?" The thought of Navarro siccing these dogs on me does more to churn my stomach than the punches.

Grolnic lets go of me. "He might have mentioned you were withholding."

I shoot a glance at Benny Chen. He looks amused. "What's funny?"

"You working for monks. Damn. Is it that bad, Landry? You're chasing Yetis and shit?"

Grolnic laughs and they head for the stairs like we've all just shared a good chuckle.

"Leave the Ghost Shadows alone," Chen tells me.

Like I'm gonna listen.

"You're muddying the waters of our investigation, and you don't want to do that. A guy in your line of work needs good relations with the O-Five." The steel door groans open and the cops tromp down the stairs without waiting for my reply.

"Hey," I yell after them, "You owe me a cigarette."

The door clangs shut on the brick box. I fetch my hat from where it landed by the low wall when they tackled me, but I don't look over the edge. My hand is still trembling when I pick it up.

◆━━◆━━◆

Lily Lao works out of an acupuncture and herb shop called The Dancing Crane on the Bowery near Confucius Plaza. I don't call ahead or drop Norbu's name when I walk in and ask for a reading. She's probably expecting me, but if there's any chance of getting a cold reading, I'll take it. I expect the place to smell like incense, but it's more of a sharp sweetness in the air like clove or cinnamon on top of tobacco. The countertop is clogged with jars of roots and leaves. Bonsai trees and bamboo plants compete for space on the cheap pine shelving with jade carvings, pot-bellied buddhas, and a porcelain Elvis. A pair of paper fans tacked to the wall are decorated with a dragon and a phoenix whose tail feathers remind me of what's in my pocket.

The proprietor, an old man in thick glasses with liver spots showing through his thinning hair, tells me that Lily is with a client. He jabs a thumb at a mahogany beaded curtain without looking away from the game on his snowy little TV. I consider leaving and not coming back, but if I do I'll only end up wondering if I missed some inadvertent clue she might've dropped about my new friend Norbu, so instead, I fidget and pace and resist the urge to have a smoke on the street. I don't want to be seen loitering in front of this place.

Ms. Lao's client—a young, pregnant Chinese woman—finally emerges through the beaded curtain. I try to get a read on her face, to tell if it was good news or bad. She looks content and shows me a shy smile. Maybe the fortune-teller is in the business of telling people what they want to hear. Most are, and I'll soon find out. Unless, of course, she tells me what my employers want me to hear. They're the ones paying for the reading, after all.

I slip through the curtain into a small room painted black like a theater set. There's a silk brocade draped table in the center and a couple of creaky wooden chairs. Lily Lao sits in one and pours herself a cup of tea while I take off my hat and settle in the other. She raises the teapot, offering me some, and I shake my head. Not a word is exchanged. She stows the teapot on a hotplate perched on a crate behind her and studies me over the rim of her gold-trimmed china cup.

"I'd like a reading," I say. She nods and sets the teacup on the table. I have to admit I've been expecting her to be as chatty as a hairdresser, plying me with questions from the get-go to gather details from which she can draw inferences about the rest of my life and why I'm here.

Most people—unless they're blowing cash on the carnival midway at Staten Island—probably only visit a fortune-teller when they're jittery about something; romance, job troubles, pregnancy. And most people with a problem wear it on their face, broadcasting their hopes and fears in how they react to questions and comments. P.I.s aren't most people.

With no chitchat Ms. Lao produces a silk pouch, opens the drawstring, and shakes three bronze coins onto the table, round with square holes in the center. When she slides the coins toward me I notice her fingernails are detailed with flowers and little rhinestones. The room is lit by electric candles in glass lotus flowers, but otherwise, it's empty of the rampant knick knacks that occupy every square foot of the storefront. The only decoration is an octagonal mirror in a white frame painted with stacks of solid and broken black lines. Combined with her silence, the austerity of the space contributes to the sense that Lily Lao is one serious character. Maybe that's part of her mystique. I guess I was expecting someone frivolous, like a gypsy. She hasn't even asked for my name. Like it doesn't matter, isn't relevant to the inner truths she's here to sift for. My heart rate ticks up a notch and my cheeks flush with embarrassment at getting caught up in the theater.

I pick up the coins and shoot her an inquisitive look.

Her accent takes me a moment to decipher when she says, "Throw the coins six times," shaking her cupped hands to demonstrate.

I follow the instructions, although I can't tell which side is heads and which is tails when they land. She marks down the results on a pad with a cheap ballpoint: a stack of solid and broken lines, like the ones on the mirror frame. After the last toss, she writes the number twenty-one next to it, then quickly dashes out a second stack of lines and the number thirty-eight.

"What are the lines?" I ask.

"Yin and yang. Sixty-four permutations to represent forces of creation. This one," she says, stabbing a finger at the twenty-one stack, "is called *Biting Through.*"

"What does that mean?"

She stirs the pen over the diagram. "Unbroken lines on top and bottom are yangs. Here they represent lips. Broken yin lines inside are like teeth. The yang in the middle is something in mouth you are biting through. It symbolize investigation."

I keep my face placid. Don't bat an eye. "What does biting something have to do with investigation?"

"To penetrate, to chew on something . . . you understand? You must cut through to the marrow and see things as they are. To administer justice." Her accent may be thick but her English is good. Her words would be impressive if Norbu hadn't sent me to her. I'm thinking, *Okay, you got my job description down. Tell me something I don't know.* "What's the other one mean? Thirty-eight."

"Not finished with twenty-one. Look: six lines. All have six lines. Every hexagram formed of two trigrams. Top here is fire. Bottom is thunder. Fire over thunder is light over sound. The fire of thunder is lightning. You are in the darkness now. To bring justice, you must illuminate. See the nature of things. Ignorant men walk into the jaws of death, but you must find truth and life at heart of the violence."

I grunt. It could mean anything.

"Second line is changing. Yin becomes yang. *Biting Through* becomes *Disharmony,* or opposition. The meaning of the changing line is, 'cutting off the nose.'"

"To spite my face?"

She squints at me. Scowls. "When the mouth eats, the nose taste the food first. Mouth by itself cannot taste much. Like this, if you have weak perception, you cannot penetrate to the deeper meaning. Is like cutting off your nose. Keeping your senses blunt. Maybe you don't want to taste the truth. Afraid of deeper forces. You walk a dangerous path. Like a blind man on a cliff. Only if you feel the wind, do you step right . . . You have been in danger today."

I remember dangling from the roof and my stomach lurches. But hey, this is all mumbo jumbo. "No shit, Sherlock," I say with a grin.

Lily Lao laughs and I can't help joining her. When it peters out, I decide to go for broke. Why not? This is all pretty opaque, and maybe it's part of her long con to make clients restless for something concrete, but I go for it anyway and throw her a bone to focus the conversation. I'm still thinking the best I can do here is steal a glimpse of what my handlers are up to, so I tell her straight up: "I'm looking for someone. Will I find him?"

She swirls the dregs in her teacup and I have to wonder if she's buying time.

"If that is what you want . . . yes."

Great, I'm talking to Yoda.

She squints at me like she's reading my aura. "You carry a heavy burden. Guilt."

Of course I do. I'm sleeping more than I did a year ago, but there are still nights when I lie awake wondering what I was doing at the exact moment when Tracy was run down by that piece of garbage in the red van. Was I pulling the trigger on my M-16 while she lay bleeding out on the crosswalk, watching the weaving taillights vanishing in the dark?

I was supposed to be the one in the path of danger during that last deployment, not her. I know it was random, some drunk they never caught. There's no divine balance sheet that made her pay for my sins. She was just too good for this shitty world. Too good for me.

I fish the peacock feather out of my shirt pocket. "I hear you can read objects. Is that right? I have something that came from the man I'm looking for."

Ms. Lao holds her palm out and I open my fist. For a second, the feather clings to my hand from static electricity. I give it a flick and it drifts down from my flesh to hers. The reaction is immediate—her eyes flash and she jerks with a little spasm. It's not from static electricity. But is it theater? She closes her eyes and strokes the iridescent barbs with her thumb. Her breathing steadies and deepens. Finally, she opens her eyes and places the feather resolutely on the silk tablecloth in front of me, finished with it.

"What did you get off it?"

She shakes her head, little more than a twitch. Scared.

My breath is shallow, my mouth dry. I tell myself I'm an asshole for letting her play me.

"The one who carried this is a beast," she says, her voice reedy and parched. "He has a mind full of blood, vengeance in his hands. But he is trying to purge his poison."

"Can you tell me anything specific about him? I need to find him, to stop him."

"Born at Mount Sinai in the Year of the Ox."

She's still staring at the feather, her face ashen. What the hell did she see?

"*How* would you stop him?" she asks, regarding the feather like it's a scorpion poised to sting.

"With the truth, maybe. With force if I have to. I do more shooting with a camera than a gun. I try to leave lethal confrontation to the police."

"Maybe you should leave it to them now."

"You think I'm in danger? Did you see that in the coins?"

"How would you stop a storm, Detective?"

I slip the feather into my coat pocket for safekeeping, open my wallet and pluck a couple of bills out. I lay them on the table. "Thank you, Ms. Lao."

"Call me Lily."

"Thanks, Lily. I'll tell Norbu you said hi."

She knits her brow at this. Or maybe it's not for

what I said to her but the last thing she says to me, "One more piece of advice, on the house. *Tao Te Ching* says, 'There is one supreme executioner. He who would take the place of the supreme executioner is like one who would cut wood in place of the master woodcarver. Seldom does he not cut his hands.'"

7

I hit a bar near Columbus Park on my way home from the Dancing Crane. Not my usual, not my favorite. I'm one of three white guys in the place and the other two are already sloppy drunk. One of these clowns—short and sinewy with a tattoo of a four leaf clover poking out the sleeve of his white tee and a drooping eyelid that looks more like a birth defect than a sign of drunkenness—weaves into me on his way to the bathroom and nearly knocks me off my stool, sloshing whiskey and ice out of my glass before it can touch my lips for the first sip.

I have time to register the clover and reflect that it's not his lucky day before a familiar dark glee overtakes me. It's like my mind just slipped from daylight into the Lincoln Tunnel, the echo of spinning tires off the tiles pulling me down through the pulsing lights into the dark place where nothing exists but this asshole's face bouncing off the floor. I'm on top of him, pummeling him, shattering his cheekbone, ripping my knuckles raw on his teeth, thinking only one thought: Tomorrow his eyes will match from the swelling; they'll *both* look droopy.

God, it feels good to unload. I almost want to thank him for giving me a reason. And then it's hands on my jacket collar, dragging me like a dog by the scruff, tossing me out into the rain, and the door banging shut behind me, cutting off an irate stream of Cantonese.

I suck on my bleeding hand, scoop up some slush from a window ledge, and pack it on the wound. It melts too fast to do much good. Even without a sip of whiskey in my system, I'm hot. The rain practically steams off me, and it isn't until I reach my apartment on Mulberry that the damp soaking through my cheap coat starts to chill me. I take the old cage elevator up to my floor, toss my wet coat on the rack, and strip on the way to the unmade bed without bothering to turn on the lights. I should piss but I'm too tired so I just crash. Next thing I know I'm back on the street.

Only it's not Chinatown, maybe not even New York. The wedge of twilight sky I can see from the narrow alley isn't cut by telephone wires but strings of ragged prayer flags. They flutter in the wind with a sound like pigeon wings. As I pass under them, the windows of the surrounding buildings pulse with the light of candles and I smell the iron tang of blood.

Rats the size of dogs scamper through puddles, their spines bowed, claws clattering as they rummage through crates of rotting vegetables. A shadow swings like a pendulum as I pass the corner where the rats have vanished in the steam and I don't want to turn my head to look at what casts it.

I force myself, and almost see the face of the skinny teen hanging from the laundry line, but my head won't turn that far. My neck burns, and looking down at what's keeping my head from turning, I see that I'm wearing a rough noose of my own for a scarf. The coarse fibers scratch at my throat and dig their splinters in. I claw at it, but it's too tight, it won't give. I can breathe, but the rope is heavy, and I trail it like a tail when I break into a run.

Frantic now, I take corners at random, splashing through oily puddles of putrid water. Rags ripple around a corner up ahead, hooves clop and echo around me. Or is that my heart?

Blood wells up through a sewer grate and floods the street. Up ahead, a steeple shining gold in the light of the rising sun flashes a beacon between the silhouettes of the buildings. Not a church, it's in the shape of an Asian *stupa*, draped with hundreds of colored flags.

I run for it, my shoes splashing through the blood, the sound of blades scraping the brick walls behind me. The piss stench of musk floods my sinuses, thick and cloying in my throat. Then the alley ends abruptly in a black iron door strapped and riveted with a giant eternal knot, and somehow I know this is an entrance to the temple I saw even though it wasn't this close just a second ago and I can't see the spire from here but I can hear the flags fluttering and the scraping sound is getting louder, the echo of hooves closer. I shove my shoulder into the iron door and it swings open.

Then it's not a door, it's a beaded curtain, and I'm inside, falling onto a polished wood floor, plunged into an atmosphere spiced with incense, ears flooded with the rich, bowel-buzzing chant of a thousand male voices.

The walls undulate with the silhouettes of swaying bodies, shaven heads bobbing in rhythm with the chant. A maroon-robed figure walks among them swinging a censer on a chain. Someone touches my wrist, places a hand gently on my back, and urges me forward, down the aisle, up the steps to a dais, to a vacant throne before a gilt statue of Yamantaka. I dig in my heels, hear the blood-lubed soles of my shoes squelching on the floor, but I can't turn away. The gentle hand in the small of my back presses me forward and I feel its long claws on my spine, hear them clacking beside my ear. The noose yanks me forward like a disobedient dog on a leash.

A whisper of blades, and locks of my hair fall into a bronze bowl. The statue reaches out with a club clenched in a golden fist and strikes the bowl. It rings like a gong, resounding in the soul I didn't know I had until the bowl is tipped over a flame and I'm choking on the fumes of my burning hair as someone whispers my new name in my ear, but I won't remember it when I wake.

✦━━╫━━✦

I peel myself out of bed, sweaty and stale, and plod into the bathroom for an epic piss. I shower, shave, and make a pot of coffee. My hand is scabbed over, crusty and brown. The details of my dreams are already burning off in the hard morning light, but I know they involved the monks and their monster. Something about a ritual, or the fortune-teller. Remembering her, I find my coat and dig through the pockets for the peacock feather. It's not much, but it's all I have to go on and I'm vaguely hoping that looking at it will give me an idea of what to do next, maybe even tease the details of my dream back from the brink of oblivion. But the feather is missing from the pocket where I'm sure I left it.

I didn't take it out at the bar, did I?

No. I'm sure I didn't.

Did Lily take it from me at our parting, with some sleight of hand? Maybe I'm being paranoid, but I feel like I need to retrace my steps and see her again. Something doesn't add up. During the session, she seemed shaken by what she got off of the feather, afraid even. She wrapped things up pretty hastily after that. But maybe her apparent fear was just a distraction.

I sit on the sofa and pull my shoes on. Tying the laces, I get a flash of them splashing through a puddle of blood. A dark alley. Streamers?

That's it. It's gone. I close my eyes and wait for more, but there's nothing. I pat my pockets again to make sure my wallet and keys are where I left them. I should know because I just dug through these pockets a minute ago, but I'm distracted, off balance. Not good.

I down the rest of my black coffee like bitter medicine. I didn't put enough water in the pot for the number of scoops I dished out and it tastes like ass.

Yeah, I'm out of the groove today.

On the street, I hoof it up to Confucius Plaza and look for the Dancing Crane logo amid the shops. The block looks different in the morning light and it takes me a minute to orient myself. Just as I'm starting to wonder if the metal is rolled down over the shop window, I notice a man in maroon opening a door and everything clicks at once. The shop is the one I'm looking for and the monk is Norbu. I'd swear to it.

I wait half a minute, then cross the street and try to spot him through the glare and clutter obscuring the store window, but I can't see inside, so I throw caution to the wind and decide to confront him. I crack the door slowly to avoid jangling the bell. On entering, I find the front room empty. The old man from last night isn't tending the counter. No one is. I smell incense, and this time I'm pretty sure it's the same weird flavor they burn at the dharma center. I slip through the beaded curtain and find myself in the room where Lily Lao read my coins last night, also vacant. The strains of a Tibetan chant reach me from a doorless opening through which I notice candlelight flickering on the corner of a narrow passage. Leaning into the corner, I can make out that it's a solitary voice. Norbu.

But where's the fortune-teller? Either she's with him, or he has a key to let himself in. In which case, there's a good chance of Lao or the old man coming up behind me while I'm creeping up on Norbu.

I berate myself for the adrenaline I feel coming on. I mean it's not like I'm infiltrating the underground gambling parlor of a gang lord. These are old school new agers, for Christ's sake. And anyway, I have a legitimate reason to be here: I'm looking for my feather. But I want to know what Norbu's up to, and I probably don't want him to know I know. That's the gig.

I head down the flickering passage, the exotic scents and sounds more present with each step. I come to a tidy stock room, the walls lined with metal shelving racks piled with boxes, jars, and a scattering of white votive candles, their wavering flames providing the only light. There's a bare bulb in the middle of the ceiling, but Norbu has chosen semi-darkness for his task. I'm grateful for it. I hide in the shadows and watch as he walks a slow circle around a square table, all the while running his mala beads through his fingers, his head swaying in a rhythmic lilt, keeping time with the chant.

What's he doing performing a Tibetan ritual here instead of in a shrine room at the temple?

At first glance I thought the table was draped with an elaborate patchwork cloth, but it's not. The colorful circle of stylized flames and tantric symbols is made of colored sand. I've come across these in my reading: A sand mandala.

I can't make out all of the details from here, but they are bountiful. Byzantine. I can tell it was no small feat to create it. Still chanting, Norbu takes a ritual implement he's been concealing in his folded palm—a small, pronged scepter—and plows it through the sand, wrecking the elaborate pattern with a straight line through its center. He's short and has to bend deep to reach across the table. For a second his eyes are aimed right at me but if he sees me, he doesn't react.

I freeze in the shadows until he moves on, and then back away up the passage. The last thing I see of the makeshift shrine room is Norbu using a brush to sweep the sand into a pile. Retreating to the front of the store through the fortune-teller's parlor, I hear the door chime. I scan for closets and exits, then drop low on my haunches and slip under the table, concealed by the silk cloth. An instant later, I see a woman's shoes and ankles enter the room. I keep my breath steady and quiet. It's crazy, I know, to be amped up in this situation, but there's something about hiding that switches all your circuits on. The shoes pause for a long moment, then continue through the side hall to the back room. Norbu's chanting has ceased, and I wonder if she'll catch him unawares, but then the indecipherable tones of congenial conversation reach me and I take that as my cue to hit the street.

Traffic is thin on the Bowery and I'm across the street before Norbu exits The Dancing Crane, clutching a brown paper bag.

He shoots a wary glance up and down the street. I step into the lee of a parked florist's van, tracking him through the front windows of the vehicle. He moves east. I trot across the street and tail him from a discrete distance.

Norbu looks back in my direction, scanning the traffic, and I can tell from his manner that it's a cab he's looking for. I duck into an alley and hope they show up in pairs, or I'll lose him.

I get lucky. Not only are two cabs coming down the street, and not too far apart, but the one in back is pulling over to drop a passenger off at the plaza. The first cab sails past me and I see Norbu hailing it. I step out of the shelter of parked cars toward the second cab, my blood pressure spiking as the old Korean lady in the back seat takes all day to get the cash out of her purse, rubbing the bills to make sure they aren't sticking together. Finally she's out and I'm in.

"Follow that cab," I tell the driver. "Don't lose him."

"Friend of yours?" Russian.

"I don't know."

Norbu's cab makes a right onto East Houston, a left onto Avenue C. Two more rights and we're on FDR Drive, heading south toward the Williamsburg Bridge. The brake lights flash and I get the feeling we're at our destination. I tell the Russian to hang back, pass him a bill that's too generous, but I don't have time to make change. Then I'm out of the cab, trying to blend into the too-sparse weekday foot traffic along the East River Park, where anyone who isn't jogging tends to stand out.

But Norbu doesn't look back. He adjusts his robe and his down vest (in matching maroon) against the waterfront wind and heads toward the river.

I follow him over the soggy ground, stuffing my hands deep in my overcoat pockets for warmth, amazed that the monk isn't shivering in his vest and thin robes. All he does is pull the top of his robe over his shaven head like a hood. I don't know if he ever lived in the Himalayas or if his people are just better built for winter, but I'm wishing I'd picked up a second cup of coffee just to warm my hands and belly. The day is raw this close to the water.

We wind along a bike path among the joggers and dog walkers to the esplanade and the gray river. The bridge looms over choppy water to the south, bisecting the park with its ugly cage and behemoth supports that resemble electrical towers. I've always thought that thing looked dangerous. Not in an unstable kind of way, just the opposite. It's probably the sturdiest bridge I've ever seen, but it has no grace, no humanity. There's an oppressive malevolence in the design.

Maybe I'm just getting caught up in all of this mystical claptrap. Monks and psychics and auras. I shake it off and come up behind Norbu at the waterfront railing. There's nothing to hide behind out here at the edge of the river. Just me and him.

He takes a black horn from his wrinkled paper bag. If I had to guess, I'd say it was an ox horn. The severed end is covered in plastic wrap secured with a rubber band. As he removes the wrapper, he starts chanting again, the syllables snatched on the wind, his robe fluttering and flapping. I watch in silence from a few feet back as he pours the colored sand into the river. It's like watching a scattering of ashes, a cloud falling into the current, blown downstream toward the bridge, grains speckling the water and sinking.

The chant swells to a crescendo and he holds out a long note at the end while digging in the bag for one more thing: *the peacock feather*. The wind tries to snatch it from his fingers, but he holds it aloft and chooses his moment to let it go. When he does, it glides up high, does a couple of loops, then drifts down to the water and disappears in the chop.

The monk turns away from the river, his face unchanging when he sees me standing there.

"Mr. Landry."

"Geshe."

"I didn't know it was your practice to follow your clients."

"Jigme Rinpoche is my client. And I don't see him throwing evidence into the East River."

"It was your idea to remove it from the crime scene. Feathers don't take fingerprints, you said."

"Why throw it away? Is that part of the ritual you were doing at The Dancing Crane?"

His face remains impassive.

"Rinpoche doesn't know about your sand art, does he?"

"No."

"Is that why you destroyed it? Was he going to find out?"

"All sand mandalas are destroyed. The practice is

an exercise in detachment: creating something beautiful, empowering it with energy, and then giving it away to the environment."

"What kind of energy are we talking about? You collected the sand in an ox horn. It's something to do with Yamantaka, isn't it? You worship the demon."

Norbu wraps his mala beads around his wrist and starts walking along the esplanade. I keep pace as he lays it out for me. "A mandala is a meditation symbol, but it is also a palace for a deity. There are mandalas for all of the tantric deities, each a vessel to house the energy of the god. I created this one to collect the energy of Yamantaka, yes. I did this in the part of the city where he has manifested as a destructive force. Then I swept it away and released it to the river to help purify the city of this energy. Do you understand?"

"I understand what you want me to believe. What does the feather have to do with it?"

"It came from the Lord of Death himself. It has a powerful connection to him. It reminds him that his poison must be transformed into medicine. On some level, he knows this, or he wouldn't have left it behind."

"Hold up. You think there's actually an ox headed *god* roaming Chinatown? Or are we talking about a man, a reincarnation, like Rinpoche suggested?"

"He is undoubtedly a man, but his bond with Yamantaka is so strong, he may take the form of the deity."

"And you think you've diffused some tension by throwing some sand and a feather in the river."

The monk chuckles. "I know this way of thinking is strange to you. Hard to have faith in what you've been told. We asked you for practical help, but this is what *I* can do. Try to help spiritually. Maybe it helps a little. One mustard seed can tip a scale."

"Does Jigme Rinpoche know you're *helping spiritually*?"

"I don't concern Rinpoche with my effort. He has more important matters on his mind."

"What could be more important than one of your demons getting off the leash?"

Norbu stops walking, looks back at me. "He is preparing for the visit of His Holiness, the Dalai Lama. You must be discrete, Detective. The situation we have entrusted you with must not jeopardize that."

"You're worried about more than bad press."

"We have powerful enemies in the Chinese government. They have ties to the tongs. We fear an attempt on Rinpoche's life, but he will take no precautions."

"Why not?"

"He doesn't want to spend resources on his own safety. He doesn't want his monks to be distracted by the need to protect him. But how can we not be? He is precious. And if Rinpoche were harmed, or even threatened . . . the Dalai Lama's visit would be canceled."

"You know, you'd be better off letting the Chinatown Monster go on killing Chinese gangsters. Let the police give them all the credit and watch it escalate. Not much time to target Tibetans with all that going on. And if there *is* a hit man with Jigme's number . . . maybe he gets taken out in the crossfire."

"We do not seek to benefit from violence," Norbu says, and I almost believe him. "Truth is the only thing that will heal the city, Mr. Landry. Keep looking for it."

I rub my hands together and blow on my fingers.

"All Lily Lao could tell me is that your man was born in the Year of the Ox at Mount Sinai Hospital. Him and a thousand others. That's not much to go on. Hell, I was born there myself. Year of the Tiger, according to all the placemats. This case is a real zoo. Lions, tigers, and peacocks. Did Lily swipe the feather off me? You ask her to?"

Is that a smile?

"Maybe you dropped it," he says.

"You could have just asked for it. You do represent my client, after all."

Now it's for sure a smile. "But then we might not have had the same discussion."

"I don't follow."

He laughs. "But you *do* follow. You followed me here. I have meditated on the feather all night and I believe the killer has a karmic connection to this place."

"*This* place? The park?"

"The park, the bridge, the river."

"Before it was a park, this was mostly slaughterhouses and shipyards. But you said your guy was a monk in Tibet last time around."

"It's just a feeling. You call that a *hunch*, right? Keep looking and you will find him."

We've been wending our way back to the street along a bike path and now that we've reached it, Norbu is signaling the end of our chat. He hails a cab.

"Word to the wise: I'm not the only one on your tail," I tell him. "Cops and gangsters will be, too, you keep poking around Chinatown."

"From now on, I'll leave the poking to you, Detective."

He bows slightly, hands folded. I touch the brim of my hat and linger on the street, watching his cab float downstream.

8

I **GRAB THE COFFEE** I've been craving and head
to my office on foot. Chinatown is quiet today, still
hung over from its New Year revels. I climb the
ill-lit stairs with my ears pricked but find no ninja
whores lurking in ambush today. Which doesn't mean
I'm lacking in female visitors; Gemma Ellison, the cute
grad student from the teahouse, is waiting outside my
door. My first thought is that she looks spooked,
sweaty around the edges.

"Ms. Ellison."

"Gemma, please."

"I'd say I'm pleased to see you, Gemma, but I get
the feeling you're not here to ask me out for another
cup of tea."

"May I come in?"

"Of course." I unlock the office door and wave her
through. She takes in the seedy but tidy environs, her
eyes lingering on the card table serving as a desk.

"You've caught me in the middle of some
renovations," I say.

"No computer?" she asks.

"Not in the budget. Maybe someday. Are you here
for my services? If you need some kind of cyber spy,
I'm afraid I'm not your man."

"Oh, no. I'm not here to hire you."

"Can I offer you some instant coffee? I don't have tea, sorry."

"No, thank you. I'm fine." She sweeps her skirt and sits at the edge of the client chair, her legs crossed. I settle in and fold my hands in my lap, waiting for her to talk first.

She clears her throat. "Miles, I don't know what kind of cases you typically handle. I mean, monks seem like pretty low-risk clients, but someone threatened me yesterday, after I spoke with you."

"Threatened you for talking to me?"

Gemma nods. She's keeping her composure but just barely.

"Who?"

"A Chinese man. Young. Big. I almost didn't come here. I came *this* close to burning your business card in the sink."

"Why didn't you?"

"Is it political? Did the Tibetans come to you because Chinese thugs are threatening them? Because if that's what this is about . . . I won't be intimidated."

Oh, Lord, she's an idealist. I sort of expected that on the surface, but here she is walking the walk. I'm equal parts impressed and disappointed: she's as brave and naive as she is pretty.

"Fact is, I don't know if it's political. I'm not sure if the monks know either. What it seems to be, so far as I can tell, is superstition. Maybe you'll disagree, seeing as you study the religion. How much of a believer are you in the supernatural?"

She tugs at the hem of her skirt, trying to decide whether or not to tell me something. I've let the conversation play out too fast, should have paced it better. Then I might have her confidence. Just when it's getting hard for me to keep looking into those big clear eyes, she shows her cards.

"I've seen monks do things I can't explain. When I was traveling in India, visiting the refugee camps. So I have a pretty open mind."

"Are you sure you didn't see whatever you saw *because* of your open mind?" I regret it as soon as I've said it. Her brow knits and I know I'm shutting her down, closing her up, the exact opposite of what I want. But I can't help myself. If she can help me make sense of this case, I have to be upfront about my skepticism.

Her eyes are turning from clear water to ice when she says, "You've got it all figured out, then? What's possible and what isn't? The nature of reality is all sorted and set for you with nothing left unexplained?"

I smirk out of habit and try to steer it toward the warmer kind of smile, but probably fail and end up looking like an idiot. "Not me, no. I just figure that smarter folks with a lot of alphabet soup after their names would have proven things like reincarnation and magic by now if there was any evidence."

"Well. You're entitled to your opinion. I didn't come here to discuss metaphysics with you." She picks lint from her skirt.

I sigh, look at my coffee, and decide not to finish it. It's getting cold and I'm feeling edgy enough as it is. "I'm sorry. I tend to play devil's advocate when I'm trying to talk *myself* out of believing in something. Can we start over?"

She fidgets in the cheap chair. "I guess."

"The last thing I want to be is dismissive. In fact, I could use your help, your expertise. So let me be of help to you first. You say a Chinese man threatened you. Where did this happen?"

"In the subway. I was waiting for my train. I was alone."

"What station?"

"Canal."

"Go on."

"I was standing near the edge of the platform when someone pushed me from behind and caught my jacket, dangling me over the tracks. He told me to mind my own business and stop talking to you."

"He said my name?"

"No. He called you 'the private eye.'"

"Then what?"

"I said *okay*. I'm not accustomed to physical threats. I was scared half to death."

"And yet, here you are. Talking to me anyway." I don't know her well enough to say how out of character this defiance is. For all I know, there *was* no threat in the subway and she's just playing her part in a game, sent here to nudge me in a particular direction. But by whom and for what? I don't have any good theories, and she doesn't feel false, but on *these* matters, I keep a *very* open mind.

The picture she's painted for me, the image of her dangling over the tracks, brings to mind my own recent brush with muscle. "You said he was big. Wide, tall, or both?"

"Both."

"And he was alone?"

She nods.

"What was he wearing?"

"Jeans, high-top sneakers, and a black jacket."

"What kind of jacket?" I'm picturing Detective Sammy Chen's motorcycle jacket, but he's not tall, not even for Chinese.

"Like a parka, a winter coat with a fur-lined hood."

"Taller than you?"

"Yes. Not by a lot, but yes, taller than me. Do you know him?"

"I don't think so. But it helps to know who I'm keeping an eye out for." Actually, I think I do know him, but I'm not telling her that yet. Big Chinese guys stand out to begin with, and the Eskimo coat seals the deal. When it comes to gangbangers, Chinese or otherwise, it's usually the more experienced and dangerous ones who don't bother trying to look the part.

"I know about the Ghost Shadows," she says. "I've seen the stories in the newspapers and on TV. Do you think the man who threatened me was one of them?"

I scratch the back of my head and glance at my hat on the coat rack. I'm itching to hit the street. "Ah . . . maybe, maybe not. They're not the only gang in town. Then you've got the tongs that the gangs work for, and the triads . . . It's as complicated as one of those Buddhist murals with all the gods, demigods, and demons."

Now she looks scared.

"Look," I say, leaning forward and steepling my fingers, "I will find out who it was that threatened you for talking to me. And I'll make sure it doesn't happen again. I promise. But can you think of why anyone—and I mean *anyone*—wouldn't want a private dick looking into the nitty-gritty of what these Tibetans are into? Or why anyone wouldn't want me working on their behalf, sniffing around Chinatown?"

She thinks for a minute. I notice her noticing the scabs on my knuckles and fold my hands in my lap under the card table. "I don't know," she says. "The Chinese government obviously has reason to want to hurt Tibetan leaders. Maybe they want to spook the Tibetans into cancelling the Dalai Lama's visit."

"Why threaten you, then?"

"I don't know. Have your monks been threatened by gang members?"

"Not yet."

She does that cute thing with her mouth, scrunching up her lips while she thinks about it. "Miles, I think if you want my help with your case, you should tell me what it's about. What exactly did they hire you to do?"

I feel my hairs going up at this. It's probably just curiosity, but what if someone *is* behind her, behind our first chance meeting? Someone who wants me to betray Rinpoche's confidence? Paranoia, right? She cares about the cause.

"When we met at the teahouse, you asked me if I was looking for a reincarnated master, remember?"

Her eyes widen. "You are?"

"Well . . . not exactly. More like a reincarnated monster."

"*The Chinatown Monster*," she whispers.

I nod.

Gemma gazes out the grimy window over my shoulder, putting it together. "Do the Tibetans think the killer is slaying Chinese for vengeance? Like a vigilante protector demon?"

I lean forward and clear my throat, drawing her eyes back to me. "They may have used some of those terms, yes. But listen to me; you're a modern American girl. There *is no* monster. He's a man, whoever's doing this. And so far, I have no reason to doubt it's just gangsters taking care of business that has nothing to do with Tibetans. They should keep their noses out of it, frankly."

"Is that what you've told them?"

"Not yet."

"But you're going to? Or are you stringing them along to collect a paycheck?"

"Hey. Look, I'm trying to help the man who hired me, but it's not that simple. You wanted to know what they hired me for and I've told you. But don't expect me to share all of my theories when we've only just met."

She nods and tucks her hair behind her ear. "That's fair, I guess."

"I'm concerned for your safety. You're sure the guy who threatened you was Chinese, not Tibetan?"

"I can tell the difference, yes."

"Well that does complicate things a little—a Chinese gangbanger taking notice of the monks and who they associate with. It might be an overreaction to my investigation, and if it is, I'm sorry for that. I poked something with a stick to see what would happen."

"Oh my god. Were you involved with that man who was hanged across the street from the tea parlor?"

"No."

"Do you think the gang leaders suspect a Tibetan of killing their guys?"

"No. But I also don't think these monks fully appreciate the retaliation they could incite by looking under rocks in Chinatown."

Gemma looks genuinely distraught.

I watch her eyes carefully and say, "Unless they really do have a monster on their side . . . "

She squints at me. "But you don't believe in monsters."

"Not the supernatural kind, no."

"You think a monk is living a double life as a serial killer?"

I think of Norbu's long fingernails, his furtive behavior. But hearing it stated so baldly . . . I chuckle, rub my scabbed knuckles across the groove between my chin and lip. "Having met some of these guys, I admit that feels far-fetched. But are they *all* like that?"

"Like what?"

"Gentle. Pacifist."

"I suppose there are exceptions and hypocrites in any religion, but more than any other I've encountered, Buddhists are non-violent. Monks take a vow not to harm any sentient being."

"What about when the Chinese invaded their country? My Asian history is a little spotty. Did they fight back?"

"At first. A little. But war would have been suicide. They had no real military."

"And what about this whole wrathful protector thing? I've been to their temple. Some of the artwork looks downright satanic. Demons flaying people, dancing on skinned corpses, and drinking blood out of skullcaps. Sexual stuff, too. How do you reconcile that with monastic vows?"

"It's symbolic of psychological processes. Energies to be tamed and channeled. You can't just repress anger and desire and expect them never to flare up. Tantric practitioners symbolize those forces and use them in the service of spiritual attainment."

"Okay. Well, at least that's consistent with what the monks have told me about it. But in all of your studies, have you come across any examples of monks taking life? Most holy books are chock full of contradiction. Does Buddha ever condone killing?"

Gemma nods in silence, thinking it over. At least bringing the conversation around to academic questions seems to have settled her nerves. I'd hoped it would.

"There is a story," she says, "about one of the Buddha's final lives before he attained enlightenment."

"So basically, we're talking mythology."

"Maybe. Depends if you're a Buddhist. Anyway, the historical Buddha, Siddhartha Gautama, who lived in India 2,500 years ago, saw all of his previous incarnations when he attained enlightenment under the Bodhi tree. The whole evolutionary chain from insect to animal to human lives. And there's a story about one incarnation in which he was the captain of a ferryboat carrying five hundred passengers. The Buddha—in this life the captain—had reached the level of a Bodhisattva. Among other things, that means that he was endowed with certain powers. He could see into the nature of things, read people's minds, and see the karmic causes and effects of different actions. Almost like precognition."

She pauses to see if I'm following or if I'm going to call bullshit on the whole story.

"Go on."

"There was a man on the ship who planned to kill everyone aboard and steal the cargo. The captain could see the evil intent in his heart, could see what was going to happen. He could warn the passengers, but he knew if he did, they would respond by killing the man, so the result of his warning them would make *them* into killers, burdening them with the evil karma of the murder, and condemning them to many lives in the hell realms."

"What did he do?"

"There wasn't much time to act. He threw a harpoon at the man and killed him before he could claim his first victim."

"A preemptive strike. Condemning *himself* to hell?"

"*Possibly.*"

"Why possibly?"

"Because the act was committed with a pure motive. He didn't kill the man out of fear or hatred, anger, ignorance, or even attachment to the lives and cargo aboard the ship. He did it to save the man from the evil karma *he* was about to incur. The Buddha chose to bring it down upon himself instead, even knowing it might set him back many lifetimes of suffering. He saw the big picture and acted selflessly."

I grunt. It's a twist I haven't heard before with regard to religious justifications for violence, I'll grant her that much. But if you don't believe in reincarnation or hell realms in the first place, the result is the same: a dead man. One who didn't do anything. Killed preemptively.

"Some Buddhists say it was a case of violence being the most non-violent course of action," Gemma says.

"Truman thought dropping atom bombs on Hiroshima and Nagasaki was the same thing. Said it saved hundreds of thousands of lives that would have been lost if the war had continued."

Gemma flinches at this. Have I made a hairline crack in the mortar of her beliefs?

"Yeah, well . . . I doubt Truman thought he was bringing hellfire down on himself, embracing damnation for the good of others when he gave the order. What happened to your hands?"

"Bar fight. Definitely not a case of violence being the least violent course of action."

"You have a temper."

I nod.

"Would you like to learn a breathing technique for controlling it?"

I manage not to laugh. "Sure."

<hr />

Soon as I've sent Ms. Ellison on her way with reassurances I won't do anything that might cause her another brush with Chinese gangsters, I grab my hat and head for the karaoke bar that's a front for the gambling operation of one Paul Tien.

I didn't give Gemma his name because if she spooks and goes to the police, I don't need them finding the wiretap equipment I've gathered from the bottom drawer of my filing cabinet and tucked into my deepest overcoat pocket before locking up and jogging down the stairs to the street.

I feel good. I probably won't get lucky and find an opportunity to hook this stuff up, but I finally have a lead. And believe it or not, I do have patience. Maybe not the patience of a Bodhisattva willing to spend lifetimes crawling up the karmic ladder from hell through the insect and animal kingdoms, but I can wait all day and night for a business to empty out before I pick the locks.

Turns out I don't have to. The place is dead, the lights off at midday when I arrive. Business—both legit and otherwise—won't start up here until nightfall. I don't love breaking into a joint in broad daylight, but like I said, patience. I canvass the little cinder block building from different angles over the course of an hour or so and decide there are no police or rivals watching it. There's a window to the basement hidden by a dumpster in the back alley. If it ever had bars on it, they've been removed, maybe to make a potential emergency exit out of it in the event of a raid. I take it as my point of entry straight into the underground card parlor.

Once I commit to the move, I get my tools out and hustle. I've got it open in less than two minutes; fairly confident the damage to the window frame will go unnoticed. There were enough scraps of trash piled against it to tell me no one ever opens it for a breath of fresh dumpster-spiced air.

I take my overcoat off, bundle it around the wiretap equipment, and toss it to the floor, then scuttle through after it. I find myself in a cluttered storage room filled with cases of soda, speaker cabinets, and microphone cables in need of repair crowding a bench with a soldering station. Karaoke does pretty brisk business in Chinatown and I would guess that Paul Tien's legit operation rivals his gambling parlor when you add in the alcohol. But that's not enough for him. It's never enough for these hustlers who defected from a commie regime for the land of opportunity.

Gemma's description of the man who dangled her over the train tracks like a mouse over a snake tank fits Paul Tien to a T. He stands out for his sheer size and don't give a damn fashion choices. If she'd seen his faded tattoos, I'd have total confirmation, but those were covered by his winter jacket. I've never had cause to bring myself to his attention, but I make a point of keeping track of the strongmen in my neighborhood so I'm not caught pissing on the wrong tree.

Word on the street is that Tien was PLA back in the motherland and that he defected during a trip to Korea. Other sources think he might still be doing work for the reds, everything from human trafficking or drug running to spying on foreign dignitaries visiting the city for UN sessions. Personally, I think the latter is a bit much for a guy who not only keeps up a legit front business but also a gambling operation and muscle for hire. Seems like government work would pay well enough to make the small-time crime superfluous, but it isn't always about the math. Some guys are compelled to capitalize on every skill they have. To do less is to leave money sitting on the table, which they can't stomach.

I put my coat back on and keep my ears pricked toward the door. The basement is silent, so I check the hall. There are two more rooms down here: the card parlor and the big man's office, which I'm surprised to find unlocked. I thought I'd have to pick it, but the only locks are on his desk drawers and filing cabinets. The desk itself is sparse, nearly empty except for a ledger and a calendar blotter, both for the karaoke bar.

There's also a cordless phone in a cradle, and that's what I'm here for. I follow the wire from the base to the jack on the wall. In a basement room like this the wire probably goes up through the ceiling, but I'll need to lift one of the water-stained acoustic tiles to find it. A quick look at his office chair on wheels tells me that standing on it is probably a bad idea.

The office has a sound system—a couple of cube speakers mounted in the corners and a subwoofer that looks big enough to suit my purposes. I unplug it, carry it over to the wall, and climb on top. I take a Maglite from my pocket, twist it on, and pop it in my mouth, lifting the tile with the top of my head, leaving my hands free to work. And there it is, the phone wire. Easy peasy. Good thing I've done this enough times to have the procedure down by rote. I could almost tap a landline in the dark, if I didn't need to see the colors of the wire jackets.

Quickly, the tools and components come out of my pockets. Wire strippers, couplers, cassette recorder, and the holy grail of cheap surveillance: a Radio Shack box designed to turn the recorder on every time the phone is picked up.

The room is cold, but I'm breaking a sweat up here in my overcoat with my arms above my head. There's a closet in the room that I keep eyeing in case I need to dash into it, but if I hear someone coming, I'm probably just gonna use the element of surprise to crash past them and hit the street.

I've got it wired in under five, the tile down, and the subwoofer back where it belongs according to the impression in the carpet. The hard part will be retrieving my gear with a comparable helping of luck, but at least now I know the lay of the land.

Back in the storeroom, I'm a little lighter, but the

window looks higher now that I have to climb out from below. I wonder how aware they are of the placement of supplies in here. Is someone going to notice if I stack a couple cases of seltzer under the window? Probably.

I'm mulling it over when I hear footsteps upstairs. Time to act. I stack the cases, knowing it's my only way out and there's nowhere to hide.

Voices in the hall, moving toward the office. Not good. This whole thing was a bad play. I'm going to leave a trail, like a goddamned amateur. Well, if that's the way it has to be, I'm going all in and make it obvious. Give them a different motive for the break-in. I scan the shelves for something of value, and thank heaven, there it is: a case of vodka still in the plastic wrap. My hand is on it when I catch a mangled fragment of conversation. I could swear I heard the word "redhead."

Are they talking about Gemma?

I almost put my ear to the door, but that's reckless and this is shaking out bad enough. When I come back to fetch my tape, there's sure to be a better lock on the window. Assuming I get out of here in the first place. I climb the cases of seltzer with the vodka in the crook of my arm, slide the window open as quiet as I can, then push the booze through. I slide it to the side, under the dumpster, leaving room for my body to follow. It's tight with my coat on and I scratch my wrists on the cement and the sharp aluminum frame, but I make it out with no one grabbing my ankles and close the window behind me. If they notice the cases of seltzer on the floor, they'll hopefully also notice the missing case of booze and think no further. If they don't, maybe I can use the window again after all.

I brush the dust off my coat, rip the plastic, and remove one bottle, slipping it into my deepest pocket where the tape recorder was before. I can't exactly go marching down Mott Street with a case under my arm, so I stash the rest under some cardboard in the dumpster and plan to come back for it later with a duffel bag.

I'm stepping out of the alley, blinking at the sunlight and adjusting my pace and posture for a nonchalant stroll down the street, when I hear the front door of the karaoke bar open and close behind me. I resist the urge to look over my shoulder but slow my stride and watch a square-shouldered Chinese goon march past me in acid-washed jeans and a suede jacket. Gotta be the guy Tien was talking to about Gemma.

I wonder if their trip to the office was for a gun hand off from one of those locked drawers, and just like that I have my next task in hand. I'm tailing him.

9

The goon takes the subway uptown. On the train I get a better look at his face and clothes. He's young but restrained, not playing up the gangster thing with jewelry, or the Chinese thing with the kind of tacky Kung Fu graphics I see the wannabes flaunting. This one looks like he's on his way to lieutenant, so he's probably on an assignment Tien won't risk on some low rank gopher. His posture shifts as we roll into Union Square, spine straightening and shoulders rolling back. I'm not surprised this is our stop. He's headed to the Diamond Path Dharma Center.

On the street, he buys a couple of hot dogs with sauerkraut and a can of Coke from a cart, then settles on a concrete planter where he can eat his lunch with a view of the dharma center from an angle that also takes in most of the path to a side entrance. I hang back and pace the street, blending in with foot traffic, watching him watch the doors and hoping Norbu won't pop out of one of them, spot me, and bring me to the goon's attention. Hell, for all I know, Tien's guy is hoping to catch sight of *me* paying a visit. He makes a few notes on a pad when monks and students come and go, but I don't see a camera, and I'm not sure what his job here is. It seems like *any* kid could have clocked this kind of surveillance, so maybe I overestimated him from the way he carried himself. But at least Tien picked someone who doesn't draw attention.

An hour and forty passes and my feet are killing me. I'm getting bored, thinking this is a waste of time. And that's when I see Gemma coming down the street, looking right past me.

I duck into the nearest doorway, a pizza parlor, and watch her cross the street until somebody grumbles about me blocking the door, and then I'm out again, hungry from the smell of food, and scanning for the goon to see if he's taking any special interest in her.

He perks up and makes a note on his pad as she enters, but that's all. If he wasn't there, I might go in after her—*fancy meeting you here*—and see what her visit's about. We both have good excuses to be visiting monks, but she didn't mention she was going to see mine today. Is she here because of me? There are two reasons I can think of for that and I don't like either: the first is the nagging suspicion that she's been keeping tabs on me for Norbu all along, but that's starting to feel wrong. The second is that she's worried enough about their safety after what I've been telling her that she can't help sounding an alarm.

Gemma is inside for maybe twenty minutes. Too short for even a meditation session. When she comes back out, she's carrying a yellow plastic shopping bag with red print. I squint but can't make out the graphics or the name on it. She heads west on 14th and I'm surprised but relieved that my new friend doesn't abandon his post to follow her.

I do. I want to know what's in that bag.

She moves fast through the lunchtime crowd, making it impossible for me to get in front of her to set up an accidental run in, me on my way *to* the dharma center. Before I can think of another approach, she's headed for the subway where I won't be able to follow without her noticing me. There's just no way around it. I'm gonna have to let this one go for now, head back to the goon maybe, or just give up on today and wait for my bug on Paul Tien's phone to roll some tape that might be worth something.

This whole gig is turning into more legwork than it's worth, considering that I'll probably have to bow out and give the monks a partial refund. The chances of me solving the murders are slim, and it was never going to be a demon incarnate anyway. Still, going home empty-handed is dispiriting. Like I'm walking away from not just a paycheck but the prospect of making peace with my past, walking away from a glimpse of what lies beyond this life. Something that might begin to heal the place where Tracy was cut out of me. It shouldn't feel that way to turn my back on hocus-pocus. I'm not in the soul hunting business. I'm a detective for crying out loud.

So what is it? What else am I walking away from?

It's the girl, of course. She's gotten under my skin and my involvement with this case is our only connection. And just as I'm thinking that and watching her descend the steps to the tunnel, she turns, as if she can sense my eyes on the back of her head.

Two things happen at once and I don't know if they're related: A hand claps down on my shoulder from behind and Gemma's gaze slides right over me without recognition. The last thing I see before I turn to face the guy grabbing me is how she pulls the shopping bag up into her folded arms, cradling it over her abdomen as she trots down the subway stairs into the shadows, and then I'm turned around, looking into the weary eyes of my old pal Detective Joe Navarro.

Did Gemma avoid me because of him? And who does she want to keep the contents of her bag secret from—me, the cops, or both? Joe's not alone. A short guy in a motorcycle jacket stands beside him, badge and hands placed on his belt, eyes cast back toward the dharma center and the goon on the planter. Detective Chen again.

"Hey Miles," Joe says, "c'mon and take a walk with us. Let's parlay."

Chen tilts his chin up 14th toward the guy with the notepad. "Real inconspicuous, huh?"

"Could be worse," I say.

"He see you?"

"No. You know him?"

Benny Chen grins. "Maybe we'll get to that. Let's walk."

10

Detectives Navarro and Chen march me down the block to the park. My stomach is growling and I'd prefer it if we could do this over lunch, but I'm too broke and it sure doesn't look like they're buying. There's some ham, mustard, and bread I can pick the mold off back in the mini fridge in my office, but for now I'm gonna have to go hungry just like all the methadone heads wandering the park. Well, at least I don't have to worry about hurling my lunch over the side of a building this time. Remembering that stunt Chen pulled on me, my palms get sweaty, and for a few heady seconds I'm overcome by the impulse to lay my hands on his shoulders and push him into traffic. The urge is bright and hot, but it passes, and now we're moving away from traffic, cutting left onto Union Square West.

It doesn't take long for the bumpy brick road to make my feet ache in these shoes, but glancing up at the rooftops, I revel in the sensation of connection to the ground. Navarro at my elbow, I follow Chen into the park toward the barking of dogs. It's a raw day, the ground crusted with slush, and we settle on a damp bench near the bronze statue of Mahatma Gandhi perched in the weeds with his walking stick, his shoulders laden with snow.

I don't care for the seating arrangements. One cop on each side means I can only read one at a time to tell if they're bluffing. Joe talks first.

"So now I've asked you politely, and he's asked you not so politely, to keep your nose out of this Chinatown Monster case. What do we have to do, Miles? Have a judge revoke your PI license for obstruction?"

"Slow down, Joe. My case has nothing to do with your criminal investigation. I'm on a private missing persons case."

Navarro scoffs. "Nothing to do, huh? *That's* how you want to play it? You're muddying the waters and you know it. I've been more than indulgent with you because we go back. But you can't show me the same respect, can you? You gotta go and abuse the friendship."

"Hey. C'mon, I—"

He raises a burly finger. "I'm not finished." He looks at my hat and sighs. "You know what I realized this week? I remember exactly when it hit me—on the crapper. I thought: Miles might be wearing Larry's hat, but he's not Larry, and you don't owe him squat because Larry wouldn't approve either, he was still around."

"Approve of what?"

"Of the way you're sullying the name of the agency he started."

"Hey . . ."

"Not reporting a murder? A murder *you* might have provoked—"

"I don't have to listen to this shit."

"Removing evidence from a crime scene . . . "

"These are *crimes*, Landry," Chen adds, "Not just

bad practices. Never mind your license, we could have you prosecuted."

I stew for a second, clenching my jaw. Joe I can take this from, but I *really* want to punch Chen in his smarmy mouth. Finally, I produce the old chestnut: "Prove it."

Chen stares at me while silence pools around our bench. It's never really silent in New York, but nobody's talking while the dogs bark and the cars honk and the trucks idle. I think of Gandhi behind us, out of view, burdened with melting snow. Man won a war for independence with peace and quiet. That doesn't seem to have worked for my Tibetan friends. Nonetheless, I'm gonna take a page from their playbook and keep my mouth shut. Mindfulness. Maybe there's something to it.

Joe gets restless. "You're telling me you didn't take a feather from Sammy Fong's body?"

"I wanted to ask the monks if it had symbolic significance. I can't tell one type of feather from another. What am I, a bird watcher? I took it, yeah. How could you know that?"

"It was a peacock feather," Chen says. "You figure that out yet?"

"Yeah."

"We found a few barbs from it still stuck in his headband," Joe says. "Now here's the money question, Miles: Was Fong wearing that feather in his headband the first time you talked to him, or only when you came back and found him cold?"

"The second."

Joe takes the hat off my head and swats me across the face with it.

"Hey!" My blood pressure spikes; I can feel it flushing up my neck as I bristle and coil to backhand the son-of-a-bitch. I want to take the vodka bottle from my coat pocket and smash it across his temple. I can see it vividly—what he'd look like on his hands and knees in front of the bench, bleeding from the bridge of his nose, shards in his eyebrow.

But I don't. Navarro may be an old army buddy, but he's still a cop and I'm shit on his shoe if they haul me in. "Feathers don't take fingerprints, Joe. It was worthless to you."

"Fingerprints aren't everything," Joe says. "We could have checked it for DNA traces, or any foreign matter that might have got caught between the barbs. You fucked up, Miles."

His forensic wet dream sounds a bit sketchy to me, but I know better than to point that out at the moment. I figure he must know it, too.

"Where is it now?" Chen asks.

"In the river."

Eyebrows rise.

"Best I can tell, a fortune teller swiped it off me and gave it to one of my monks who tossed it in the river." I shrug, leaving Norbu's little back room ritual out of this summary. Not sure why I'm protecting him; it's not like he's even exactly my client, but Joe and Benny Chen are holding more cards than I realized, and holding something back just feels like good strategy. "What can I say; I'm working for a bunch of superstitious nuts."

"Fortune teller, eh?" Chen says. "Got a name?"

So they're going to squeeze her? Whatever. Maybe they'll get more than I did. "Lao Liu. Goes by Lily. Works out of a shop called The Dancing Crane."

"Lao?" Chen asks.

"Yeah, you know her?"

Silence from both.

"Come on, guys. I'm helping you at great risk here. What do you have for me?"

"Great risk," Chen says. "What, the monks gonna rough you up?" He starts harping on the refrain about how not arresting me for tampering with a homicide scene should be plenty when Joe cuts in: "The kid you were watching scope out the dharma center, his name is *Henry* Lao. He's Paul Tien's top guy."

"Lotta Laos in Chinatown," Chen says.

"He's the fortune teller's son?" I ask.

"Dunno," Joe says. "But I will soon. Even if there's a connection, it's a moot point to you, Miles, since you're dropping your case."

"I never said I was dropping it."

"You want to drop it. Trust me. You don't need this client."

"I need to keep the lights on and eat. This is what came to me. What's it matter to you if a bunch of monks want to burn money sending me to chase phantoms?"

Joe rankles. "Don't give me that. You might *think* you're chasing phantoms, but you're rubbing elbows with monsters. Guys who commit murder when you knock them into each other. Take the advice while I'm offering it on a park bench and not at the precinct. You don't need to be an accessory to what these guys are into."

He's not talking about gangsters, is he? He's talking about the Tibetans.

"Do you know something about my client?"

"Wish you'd stop calling him that."

"Lemme guess: You had a run in with Norbu."

Chen takes a spiral pad from his jacket pocket and flips through it.

"His interest in the Chinatown Monster doesn't look good. So we followed him."

"He's not the man who hired me. He's just a secretary to a man too old and frail to be a killer."

"Maybe this Norbu does more than set up meetings for his boss," Joe says.

"You think Norbu is the Chinatown Monster? A Buddhist monk."

"I never said that."

"Why would the monks hire me to look into the murders if they're the ones responsible?"

"Maybe they want you to alert them to evidence, vulnerabilities, places the police might look," Chen says.

"Or tip them off to what the police know because you have friends on the force," Joe says.

"They're not that crafty."

"You sure?" Joe asks.

"What did you find on him?"

Chen reads from his notepad. "ST Circus was the codename of a CIA training operation for the Tibetan Freedom Fighters in 1959. They took Tibetan guerrillas, some of them former monks, to Colorado and trained them as paratroopers, then dropped them back into Tibet from B-17 bombers under cover of darkness to cause trouble for the invading Chinese army. They also airdropped crates of arms and supplies to support warriors on horseback. It didn't amount to much in the end, but the CIA spent almost two million dollars on the Tibetan resistance in the sixties before Kissinger shut it down so Nixon could shake hands with Mao."

"What does any of that have to do with Geshe Norbu?"

"He was researching it at the New York Public Library," Joe says.

"How do you know that? You squeeze a librarian?"

"You telling me you couldn't get inventive if you wanted to know what somebody was reading and Xeroxing?"

"So he's interested in his country's history. These monks are preserving a dying culture."

Joe gives me a dark look. "He's interested in an elite group of warriors, a notable exception to his country's pacifism, who were trained to kill Chinese. That doesn't give you pause?"

"Yeah, I get it, but it's academic. It doesn't make him guilty of anything. And it's history. We're talking about 1959. Did they actually kill any Chinese?"

"Who knows? The CIA probably doesn't even know. They probably dropped them in and hoped for the best. I think most were killed. But a guy who is fascinated by this event and also interested in these Chinatown killings . . . is probably not the meek and mild tofu muncher you take him for."

"I appreciate the tip."

"Back out of it, Miles," Chen says.

"We're asking you as friends," Joe says.

"Sure."

I nod and grin. My stomach growls. I put my hat on and go looking for a bite.

Back at the office I wrap the last piece of mold-free bread around the ham, squeeze a mustard packet into the fold, and tuck in. With better mustard, this might almost taste like food. I toss the rest of the bread in the trash so I'm not tempted to eat it and pour myself a short glass of the vodka I filched from Paul Tien's karaoke bar. I add a splash from a dusty bottle of flat ginger ale and sit down at the card table that's still serving as my desk to watch the blinking red light on the phone dock while I eat. It gives me a little shot of hope, that light, and I like to prolong that hope, draw the feeling out so I can savor the possibility that it represents new business. It improves my lunch.

Ice and Dijon. Two simple amenities that would significantly upgrade my dining experience. I put them out of my head as I chew the last bite and wash it down. Then I brush the crumbs from the table and poke the play button beside the red light with my index finger.

The voice is Lily Lao's. I only get the gist of her message on first listen. On the second, my ear is tuned to her accent—it's stronger than when she did my reading the other night, which I attribute to stress—and I'm able to fill in the words I missed the first time.

"Mr. Landry, this is Lily Lao from Dancing Crane. I read your fortune, you remember? I need to see you. Soon as possible. Something I need to tell you about your feather and your future. Very important. Okay, call me."

The next message is also from her. "Mr. Landry,

Lily Lao again. I don't want you to think I'm trying to make money on another reading. Please call me or come to shop when you get this. I'm worried about my son."

Small world. The goon I tailed this morning *is* the fortune-teller's son. My hand hovers over the handset, but I stop myself from calling her back. Navarro and Chen are probably at her shop right now. I practically sent them there. Or Chen is, anyway. Joe? Probably not. He's not officially on the case; it's my involvement on the periphery that dragged him in. Our park bench chat was a favor he did Benny Chen as someone with a little leverage over me.

Periphery? Don't kid yourself, Miles. You're swirling around the center of this thing, whatever it is. And maybe you're *the one Joe's doing a favor, pulling you out by the collar.*

I grab my coat and hat and lock up. If I call The Dancing Crane, Chen might see my number come up or overhear me talking to Lao. If I just show up, I can scope out the situation from the street and hang back until he leaves.

A few theories bang around my head as I hoof it over to Confucius Plaza. Maybe she's calling me *because* Chen showed up asking her about the feather. Maybe my tailing of her son wasn't as discrete as I'd thought and he told her about it. Why that should get her worked up into a panic, I can't fathom. It's not like I witnessed him doing anything criminal. No, she sounded like a woman afraid for her son's life. He's obviously entangled with criminals, but my gut tells me that hasn't scared her much before now. For some reason, she suddenly thinks he could be the next target of the Chinatown Monster. The question is why? Because she took the feather from me that I lifted off Sammy Fong's corpse?

The Dancing Crane looks as dark and unpatronized as ever, with the CLOSED sign facing outward in the window. Through the plate glass I don't see anyone at the counter. I scan the parked cars on the street for hints of Benny Chen or anyone else that smells like pork. Nothing.

Without thinking about it, I find my hand dropping into my pocket for my leather gloves, slipping them on. Something tells me it's dangerous to be here, dangerous to leave a trace. Maybe it's the echo of her voice on the phone in my mind, the tone of fear. I reach the door at a brisk pace, find it unlocked, and slip into the dark interior with the bell heralding my arrival.

I listen for voices, but the shop is quiet.

I draw a breath to call her name and hold it. The place smells like a slaughterhouse, the tang of blood heavy in the air, overpowering the residual spice of incense.

I draw my gun and step through the beaded curtain into the reading room. She's not there. The little table we sat at together is turned on its side, the silk tablecloth spilled in a tangle on the floor, the I Ching coins scattered amid shards of silvered glass. A glance at the wall confirms that the octagonal mirror was knocked off the wall and shattered in a struggle.

I think of the unlocked front door and the CLOSED sign. The door would be locked if they were closed. Either someone had a key, or Ms. Lao opened the door for someone she knew. Someone who waited until they were through the curtain and out of view of the street to strike.

Gun raised, I creep down the narrow side hall to the stock room with a mounting sense of déjà vu. Before I reach the end of the hall, I can tell by the pulsing golden light that I will find the room lit by candles on the shelves, just as it was the last time I was here.

There's a body draped over the table in the center of the room, the table upon which Norbu created and destroyed his sand mandala, the symbolic fortress of Yamantaka, Lord of Death.

I flip the light switch, sweep the room with the muzzle of the gun and find it devoid of the living. The bare bulb throws its ugly white light down on the scene, making the room too red for my head.

The vodka soaked sandwich rises in my gullet. I taste mustard and bile before I choke it back down. I can't have my DNA splattered all over the corpse of this woman who called me twice in the last hour. But I almost lose it. The heat is cranked, and in my coat and gloves, I nearly faint. I've never been squeamish, but the cloying air is too much, the sickly thickness of melted wax and clotting blood, the grinning gash across her throat from ear to ear, and the vertebrae I can see glistening like a pearl in an oyster. I'm on my knees before I know it, my gloves slipping in the blood on the concrete, my nose level with the table, the body, and the shard of mirror that did this.

For a terrible moment, I'm sure I'm gonna puke. Scenes from Panama flicker around my brain like flashbulbs. Women and children.

Lily Lao's eyes are open, staring through me. She made a vocation of pretending to see mysteries, but it hits me now that she knew the identity of the

Chinatown Monster *before* he showed up at her parlor. Was it her son? Norbu? It doesn't matter, he's gone, but I'm still here, and it is slowly sinking in—as the blood soaks through the knees of my pants—that *I'm still here* and Detective Chen is probably on his way to interview the dead woman.

My gun. I dropped it when I went down. I retrieve it from under the table and holster it, grateful it didn't land in the blood pooling on the floor. On my feet again, I give myself the once over. If there's blood on my black overcoat, it blends in. I button the coat to hide the stains on the knees of my gray slacks, and stare at the palms of my gloves in horror. Taking a step back, I'm granted the slight relief of finding no prints from my shoes.

There's a steel door between the shelf racks that I didn't notice by candlelight. The kind with a bar latch. Probably lets out on a back alley. I elbow the light switch back down, tug my gloves off and stuff them in my pocket, then tiptoe around the blood puddle to the door. I hip check the bar and step out into cold, clean air and daylight, leaving the candlelit horror for the cops.

11

In the basement of my apartment building, I remove the buttons and zippers from my coat and pants before burning the clothes with my gloves in the furnace. It takes longer than I expected to reduce it all to ash, and all the while I worry I'm making a grave mistake. You can go to the cops about a body you found right up until you start destroying evidence. But having started down this path, I drop the buttons and zippers down a storm grate on my way to the bodega down the street for a bottle of ginger ale, a bag of ice, and a microwave dinner. The temperature plunged with the sun, and I'm shivering in my old Army jacket when I get back to the lobby with the grocery bag swinging from the raw bare hand that isn't stuffed in a pocket. I'm gonna need new gloves.

The phone rings while I'm eating and working on my second drink. I'm expecting it to be Joe Navarro calling from the lobby, but it's not. It's Gemma.

"Miles? I hope you don't mind me calling you at home. I got your number from directory assistance."

"Not at all. What can I do for you?"

"A man was following me after class, I think."

"What did he look like?"

"Chinese, athletic. I guess he could have been a student, but . . . "

"You think he was a gang member."

"I don't know."

"Where did he follow you to?"

"I um . . . didn't go back to my apartment because I didn't want to lead him to it. I think I lost him."

"This was just now? Where are you calling from?"

"A pay phone on campus."

"You're afraid to go home."

"That's silly, right? Paranoid? I'm sorry."

"Considering recent events and the company you keep, it's neither."

"You mean Tibetans?"

"I was thinking of me, actually. But if you're not worried about that making you more of a target, I could meet you and walk you home."

"Would you?"

She gives me the location and I take a cab up to West 116th in Morningside Heights. She's waiting for me at a cafe bustling with Columbia students and faculty. I comb the room and the surrounding streets before approaching her, but find no sign of the late Lily Lao's Ghost Shadow son. Gemma looks relieved to see me. She offers to buy me a bite in return for the escort, but I tell her I already ate. After that TV dinner, I could eat again, but I'm not sure what I'd order in a place like this with a California menu. Anyway, I'd feel weird about letting her pick up the tab.

She wraps her scarf around her neck and in a little while we're walking through Harlem toward her place. It's cold, but not as bad as it's been. Heavy clouds trap the city light and cast it back down at the streets with a jaundiced glow. If anything falls tonight, it'll be rain, not snow. Gemma makes a few stabs at small talk, but I respond with one word answers and grunts. After a few blocks, she catches on to my vigilance and quiets down, letting me scan the doorframes and alleys in silence.

Eventually, we arrive at a four-story brick walk-up that looks like most of its neighbors. She digs in her purse for her keys.

Inside, she goes ahead of me up the stairs, her skirt swaying almost at eye level. I hustle up beside her and train my eyes on the upper stairs. It's an echoing tile stairwell with metal handrails painted institution green. A moment of keys rattling and we're in her apartment.

I feel like I've just stepped into the Diamond Path Dharma Center. A string of paper prayer flags is draped corner to corner across the small living room and the walls are hung with tapestries between shelves of bric-a-brac, including statues of buddhas and deities, most of them small but rendered with detail and presence. Gemma waves at a futon propping up a pair of throw pillows embroidered with beadwork elephants. "Make yourself comfortable. Would you like a glass of wine?"

"Sure."

She vanishes into the kitchenette. I consider going after her to help open the bottle, but a glance tells me it's tight in there and I don't want to crowd her. Not yet, anyway. Then, turning around, I see the yellow shopping bag with red print that she was carrying this afternoon when she left the dharma center. It's sitting on the floor beside an end table as if she dropped it there before going to class and hasn't had time to put away the contents. The name on the bag: POTALA ARTS.

From where I sit on the edge of the futon, the bag is just within reach. I hesitate until I hear the cork pop, then reach over and peek inside the bag to the sound of wine glug-glugging into a glass.

Empty.

No. There's a handwritten receipt.

$$Phurba\ \$9.00$$
$$Tax\ .63$$
$$\$9.63$$

I recognize the word. Most of the recent studying I've done has gone through my head like water through a sieve, but this is a term I saw in a glossary. The word for a ritual dagger. It stuck in my filter as another oddity of this peaceful religion.

So someone at the center bought one and gave it to her. Why? And where is it now?

I close my hand around the receipt and tuck it into my jacket pocket as Gemma emerges from the kitchenette with two glasses of wine. She passes me one, and we toast. "Long life," she says. It's a deep spicy red. I'd guess Pinot, but I'm no connoisseur. We sit down and I set my glass on the end table. The color reminds me of the fortune-teller's blood.

It's been a long day and I should be going now that I've seen the grad student safely home, but the fact is I'm glad she asked me in. I'm grateful to take refuge from the Fifth Precinct boys bound to be banging on my doors and ringing my phones tonight.

Gemma nods at my army jacket and says, "What happened to your overcoat and fedora? You so looked the part in them."

"Coat's at the cleaners and this old thing doesn't go with the hat."

"Were you in the army?"

"Two tours then retired."

"Retired? How old are you?"

"Almost thirty."

"Huh."

"What?"

"I thought you were older. Maybe it was the hat. Funny how age difference matters less as you get older."

"Matters less for what?" She's close to me, her eyes big and deep, her shoulder touching mine. She smiles and I kiss her lips, lightly.

I don't ask how old she is. She's in college, in her twenties. That's all I need to know. She tastes like wine. "I thought Buddhists didn't drink," I say. Her brow furrows and I regret the comment, but then she grins again. Her eyes look drowsy and dreamy and I wonder if there will be a second kiss. She's had a stressful evening. She might just fall asleep on me.

"Told you, I'm only about seventy-five percent Buddhist."

"On a good day, as I recall. Is today a good day?"

"Maybe." There's a tease in her tone.

"And the other twenty-five is pagan, right?"

"And agnostic. Usually. Tonight I'm feeling at least thirty percent pagan. So maybe it's a good day for *you*."

I lean in and kiss her again, more urgently this time. Her tongue darts across my upper lip and when the kiss breaks I want the talking to be over but a tenacious part of my brain—the problem solver who doesn't care about my body's needs and how tight my pants are getting—recognizes this as an opening to ask about the dagger. I try to push it down, but it won't stay down. Once that part of me pricks up, it just has to probe for an opening.

"You said Tantric Buddhism is part pagan anyway."

She leans back and regards me with exaggerated surprise. "I've discovered a mythical beast: a man who listens."

"In my line of work, a man has to. What did you mean by that, anyway? The monks are stricter than Catholics, right? Celibate *and* liquor free. At least a priest can romance the bottle."

Gemma's elbow rests on the futon back beside my ear. She wraps a lock of my unruly black hair around her finger. "The tantric Buddhists aren't always restrained by those vows. They can channel sexual energy into their meditation practice. Wrathful energy, too. But those are advanced practices for students who have taken Vajrayana initiation. They meditate on detailed paintings of goddesses and demons, chant secret mantras under the supervision of a guru. It's dangerous."

"Dangerous how?"

"The energy can become unbalanced. It's easy to fall off the path and trick yourself about your motives. And channeling too much energy at once could damage the body or mind. It's a crucible under pressure; it can crack. The personality can shatter. But they say tantra is the fastest path to enlightenment."

"Hmmm. Monks with pornographic paintings and demon protectors . . . It does sound pagan. I've even read about ritual daggers."

"Thangka paintings are *not* pornographic. And the daggers are symbols."

Her dreamy demeanor has given way to something with sharper edges. I've bumbled with her switches and dials and she's defaulting to cerebral mode, but I'm no closer to knowing about that dagger. I try to steer us away from the rocks, back out toward the swelling waves we were riding a moment ago. I place my hand on her thigh, but my rough skin snags on the sheer fabric of her skirt. "I came across some books on tantric sex in my research. Sounds like the ecstasy comes from going slow. Holding back."

"That can work." It comes out in a whisper.

"I'm sure there's more to it. You need a good teacher, right?"

"Teacher isn't the same as partner. In Tibetan tantra, the monks usually focus on an imaginary consort, a visualization."

"But some do it with a real woman?"

"Some. Advanced yogis visualize their partner as a *dakini*."

"What's that?"

"A goddess. They worship her as an embodiment of the wisdom mind. Union with her opens the mind, and brings . . . bliss."

We kiss for the third time, sliding down the back of the futon until she's on her back and I'm on top of her and we're done talking.

<hr/>

She straddles me on the bed, her sweat-slicked body

grinding in the candlelit currents of incense, her face hidden in the fiery cloud of her red hair. I'm on the brink, riding a wave that's been cresting forever, when she whips her head around, whirling the mane away from her face. My heart skips a beat at what flashes through her paper-pale skin: red flesh and a third eye, bared fangs, and a necklace of skulls. My fingers clenching her ass lock up as I spasm and she rakes her claws down my chest. Suddenly, her body is wreathed in curling flames and my dog tags rise toward her scarlet breasts, straining on their beaded chain, forsaking gravity for her magnetism.

The vision lasts for less than a second and then it's gone.

It's Gemma again, only Gemma, her eyes squeezed shut and mouth open, face contorted with ecstasy, body wracked with tremors. She washes over me like a crashing wave, her sweaty hair falling in a curtain around my face. I catch a glimpse of something bronze on the dresser beyond the candles—a triangular spike with a demon-headed pommel protruding from a wooden base. The *phurba*.

I'm drifting off already, going soft inside her, awake enough only to wonder if I'm already dreaming. Was there something in the wine? And then I'm sure of it: I'm dreaming.

+ —— + —— +

In a dirty alley again with the smell of piss. Tattered prayer flags overhead where laundry lines should be, and the clop of hooves on asphalt closing in. Ahead, the spire of a temple blazes in the setting sun, a beacon of gold amid the gray skyscrapers. In the bowels of the street, I feel more than hear the droning of monks chanting. It rumbles through the ground like a subway train passing. The soles of my shoes feel tacky, clinging to the pavement as I walk toward the spire, and I don't look down, but I know it's congealing blood I'm walking through.

I pass graffiti-stricken brick and a mosaic of mirror fragments stuck in a cement wall. My face fractures, kaleidoscopic, eyes too far apart. The hooves are getting closer. The scraping of steel on brick sings to me.

A gentle wind rises, sending scraps of paper and trash scudding past my legs. It carries a voice: *Khye-rang go tshen-la ga-re zhu-gi yö?*

With the wind comes fog and the tang of the river, a faint odor of burning hair, and I know that I have dreamed this dream before. Did the beast catch me last time? Have I seen its shape? Or did I escape into the temple?

It's too far away, the sounds too loud. There's no escaping now.

A figure emerges from the fog over my shoulder, lumbers forward, horns and arms outstretched toward the alley walls. I move to evade its grasp and my back touches a wall—a dead end that wasn't there a second ago. I fumble in my jacket for my gun, but the shape my fingers find in the shoulder holster isn't the familiar buffalo grip, it's a shaft of cold metal, oddly carved. I withdraw the weapon and my eyes confirm what my hand already knows—it's a *phurba*.

My pursuer's ox-headed mask hovers over my shoulder, as if sniffing fear from the hollow of my collarbone. All the little hairs on my body rise.

The wearer of the mask blows smoke through the

nostril holes, woody and spiced, and it soothes me, body and mind.

The masked figure speaks again. I don't understand Tibetan, but the inflection tells me it's a question. "*Khye-rang go tshen-la ga-re zhu-gi yo?*"

"I don't understand. Who are you?"

The figure raises its hands, but they aren't holding blades after all. The scraping sounds were steel claws jutting from the fingertips of hide gloves. It touches its face and lifts the mask to reveal the face of Jigme Rinpoche. His leathery skin breaks into a mischievous smile, and he asks the question a third time, in English: "What is your name?"

12

I WAKE UP ALONE, morning light slanting through blinds, whispered words in Tibetan tumbling through my addled brain, and for a good half a minute I have no idea where I am. I've only seen this room by candlelight and it's alien at first until my eyes find the deformed candle stumps, the ash trail of incense on a silver burner supporting the charred end of an exhausted stick, and the hilt of the *phurba* jutting out of its triangular base like a demonic birthday candle in a wedge of cake.

The smell of coffee finds me, and I get out of bed, feeling grungy and sore, find my boxers on the floor and put them on before following the scent. I almost forego my tank undershirt, thinking I'll hop in the shower soon, anyway, but it's chilly now that I'm out from under the sheets, so I tug it on as I step into the living room.

Gemma is in the kitchenette, washing a pan by the window. Another cold, gray day looms beyond her, backlighting her frizzy hair as she turns and smiles at me.

I clear my throat and mumble a good morning. She nods at the coffee pot, tells me where to find a mug, and asks if I like scrambled eggs. I pour a steaming cup, tell her sure, and take a seat at a metal trimmed Formica table that looks like it belongs in a 50s diner. Running my finger along the trim, I wonder if the table came with the apartment.

"You have class this morning?"

"Not until eleven."

I hear propane firing, butter sizzling, a wire whisk clattering against Pyrex. The sounds and smells of domestic bliss. And for a moment, I wonder wistfully if they will ever be the sounds of my daily routine. By the time Gemma brings me a plate of eggs and toast, the caffeine is flipping my switches, and my questions are right where I left them last night.

"Sorry, no sausage or bacon," she says. "I'm mostly vegetarian."

"S'okay." I tuck in. It's good, and the notion that she put something in my wine last night seems crazy and paranoid now.

"You sleep okay?" she asks.

"Mmm. Weird dreams." I neglect to mention that I had one of them while we were screwing. Would I know if I was dreaming right now? All of the boundaries in my life are feeling blurry. Maybe the coffee will sharpen them.

"What's on the investigative agenda today?" She sits across from me and sips her OJ.

I shrug. "Walkin' and talkin' like usual. See what shakes out." I can't help the feeling that whatever I say will make it back to the monks. Fact is I plan to confront Jigme Rinpoche today, tell him I'm not interested in being a pawn in whatever game he's playing. It'll be nice if I can do that before the police give me my daily squeeze, this time regarding the murder of Lily Lao. But as soon as these thoughts form, I can't help wondering where Lily's son is today and what my tape has picked up from Paul Tien's phone. My wiser half may be sure I'm dropping the case, but my curiosity hasn't got the news yet. Or is curiosity a cheap motive to pin it on? Have I slipped onto a different track without noticing? Am I in it for the pursuit of truth and justice, those elusive intangibles so seldom cashed in? I never got either for Tracy. Nobody saw the plate number. Mr. Red Van is still out there somewhere, probably still drinking and driving. You'd think if anybody could have tracked him down, it would be a private detective, right? But that trail was stone cold long before I got back to the States. Some days I'd like to believe in karma, to think I've bloodied him in some random bar fight by now, or that he's wrapped his truck around a tree on the L.I.E. But that's just wishful thinking.

When I snap out of these musings, Gemma is studying my face, wondering where I went. So I do what I always do when I feel vulnerable: I go on offense.

"You've got quite a collection of Tibetan art and knick-knacks," I say, waving my fork at the living room.

Gemma nods. "I'm lucky to live in Manhattan, given my interests. There are so many importers and shops run by immigrants who know their stuff."

"I noticed the *phurba* on your dresser. That's a ritual tool, right? I thought you were an academic, not a practitioner."

Is the thin line of her mouth going tight and bloodless or is that my imagination? She could have hidden the dagger if she didn't want me to see it. As it is, I'm just grateful she didn't reach for it and plunge it into my chest at the height of the festivities.

"I like to surround myself with the symbolism."

"Yeah, you said last night that the ritual tools are symbols. What did you mean by that?"

Gemma sighs. Maybe it's too early for a lesson on tantra. But she indulges me. "The *phurba* is technically a dagger, but it isn't used to cut anything physical. Buddhists inherited it from the shamanism of the Kathmandu Valley."

"Shamanism?"

"The local paganism. Vajrayana Buddhism and Bon Po Shamanism have roots in the same soil. Some scholars say the *phurba* evolved from tent spikes, or the stakes nomads used to mark the corners of fields to show lordship over an area. Others say it represents the world axis or the Shiva lingam."

I flatten my hand and pass it over my head. Gemma laughs.

"Lingam means penis. So: *penis of the god*. Symbol of creative force. Buddhists, as I think I've mentioned, don't exactly believe in gods in the usual way. Still, they inherit a lot from Hinduism, just like Christians inherit a lot from Judaism."

"What *did* Buddha have to say about gods and devils?"

"When asked if they exist, he basically said *what difference does it make?* The supernatural wasn't his concern. He was more focused on what he could teach the living about the causes of suffering and the practices for transcending it. In his view, gods, if they existed, didn't really matter because obviously they couldn't alleviate man's suffering. We can only do that for ourselves."

"So a Buddha can't save you?"

"No. He can only teach you how to save yourself, how to sever the roots of your suffering and purify your own karma. He can't do it for you."

"Severing the roots of suffering. Does the dagger symbolize that?"

She looks genuinely surprised at the insight. "You're a quick study. Yes, it may have come down from shamans who took gods and devils more literally, but in the hands of Buddhists, the *phurba* is a symbol of cutting through negativity, attachment, and obstacles to enlightenment."

It all sounds so rational in the light of day. "So why do *you* have one?"

She sits up and waves her hand over the table, as if clearing away the clutter of her academic explanations. "Okay. I *could* say some crap about how we all need the psychological tools to cut through negative attitudes . . . but it wouldn't be the simple truth."

"Which is?"

She bites her lip and shrugs. "I'm superstitious. I got spooked by everything that's been happening and I wanted some spiritual protection in my home. An amulet to ward off evil. So I bought it at a Tibetan arts shop and asked the Rinpoche to bless it."

I laugh.

"You think I'm silly. I knew you would."

"No, I don't. Really. It's just . . . most people would have bought a gun for home defense. You buy a symbolic dagger that probably can't even cut anything."

She shrugs. We both laugh and the tension eases.

"Jigme, he thought it would help?"

"He humored me. I'm not initiated into the ritual practice, but he probably thought if it gave me some peace of mind, why not?"

"And if the Chinatown Monster was a real demon, and he came knocking down your door . . . Would it help then?"

"Probably not. But why would he ever come for me?"

13

When I arrive at the dharma center on West 14th, there's a plainclothes cop watching the entrance. Caucasian, buzz cut, I can just tell. And I don't think he's there waiting for a monk. It's me they want to talk to and I haven't been home or to the office. In my old jacket and lacking the trademark hat, I'm almost in disguise but there's also nothing to hide my face so I duck into a corner store and buy a Yankees cap. There goes my lunch money. But with the bill pulled down, I'm able to blend in with the crowd on the street and slip up the garden path on the side of the building without getting collared.

The side entrance puts me in the lobby with its high ceiling and art gallery atmosphere. I can see the cop on the street through the glass of the main entrance, the etched eternal knot superimposed over his restless form. At the front desk, where I expect to find Norbu manning the phone, I find a skinny young monk in glasses—one I haven't seen before. I give him my name and tell him I'm here to see Jigme Rinpoche. He asks me to wait and strides down the hall, disappearing through the slit in the curtain that leads to the main shrine room where the holy man first pitched me the job. I don't hear any chanting, so presumably I'm not interrupting a liturgy.

The young monk reappears less than a minute later and waves me through. "Rinpoche is expecting you," he says with a smile.

Beyond the curtain, I find Jigme Rinpoche sitting on a meditation cushion in the same spot he occupied at our first meeting. The room is lit by slanting rays of dusty sunlight and a flickering row of butter lamps on a low table at the base of the big Buddha statue. The painting of Yamantaka catches my eye, but today there are no offerings laid out before it.

It's just the two of us in the room together and the air is thick with the heat of the little flames. There's no one to instruct me in the proper protocols and etiquette this time, but I feel like I should offer a gesture of respect. I've been considering the prospect that this man is a puppet master, possibly a murderer, but the sight of him with his warm smile and frail body makes me feel like an idiot. Still, history is full of charming old men pulling the strings of killers. I bow awkwardly and look around for a cushion to sit on, but he knocks the breath out of me by rising to his feet in a fluid, twisting motion that's almost gymnastic.

"How are you?" he asks.

"Fine, thanks. I was in the neighborhood. Thought I'd check in."

"Good, good."

"Where's Norbu?"

"Running errands. I read about another Chinatown murder in today's paper. A woman this time. So sad. What do you think? Is it related to the others?"

I clear my throat. "It would seem so. What did the paper say? Are the police suggesting it's related?"

He raises an eyebrow. "You haven't read the paper? The police still say everything happening in Chinatown is from gangs. But the reporter thinks maybe a serial killer. This woman . . . no one can say if she is connected to gang members."

I scoff at this. "Rinpoche, the way gangs work is that *everyone* in a neighborhood is connected to them. They ask for money to protect you from rival gangs, and then threaten to burn your shop down if they don't get it. They want a piece of every pie."

For a moment, I feel like he's giving me an MRI with his unblinking eyes. Then he says, "So you believe she was killed by a gangster, not the Chinatown Monster?"

"How do you know they're not one and the same? I mean this doesn't seem to have anything to do with your people." I'm testing him now. I know full well that Norbu had a connection to Lily Lao. He sent me to her. But does Rinpoche know that?

He turns away from me and approaches the painting of the ox-headed demon with three eyes and a fan of arms grasping a wheel of weapons in clawed fingers. "Remember: *this* is who we are looking for."

"We. Norbu is poking around Chinatown. I thought that was my job."

The old monk picks up a stack of small brass bowls. One by one, he lays them out in a row in front of the painting and pours water from a pitcher, filling each to the brim. He works slowly and doesn't spill a drop. A water offering to the deity. I've read about it. But this beast looks like he'd rather drink blood than water.

"Norbu is my eyes and ears. I need to see things from many angles to form a clear view." He fills the last bowl and sets the pitcher down on a shelf. I can't see his expression.

"The woman who was killed," I say, "Have you talked to Norbu about *her*?"

Rinpoche turns to face me, his eyes glistening. "He is heartbroken for her."

"So you're aware that he knew her."

"Yes. She had some skill with Tibetan divination. Mo dice and mirror gazing."

"Did you know that Norbu made a sand mandala in the back room of her shop, where her body was later found?" I can feel the heat rising in me, hear it curling the edges of my words.

Rinpoche's eyes narrow. "You said you didn't read the paper. Yet you know a lot about this murder. Did the police talk to you about it?"

"You didn't answer my question."

He changes the subject. "If it is, as I suspect, a reincarnated monk killing these people . . . he is tragically deluded."

"Norbu suggested that the killer is trying to protect you."

"From a fortune teller?"

"Maybe she knew the killer's identity. Or, to take your worldview all the way, maybe *she* was a reincarnation of a Chinese soldier who massacred monks, nuns, and children."

He studies my eyes like a jeweler searching for flaws. "Reincarnation is not limited by race, Detective. Next Chinese gangster you meet may have been your mother once, may have nurtured and cared for your needs when you were helpless, yes? Over thousands of lifetimes, why not? Maybe you owe him a debt."

I don't know what to say to this. He continues, "The killer has forgotten this. He needs to remember. All life is precious. This has gone too far."

"I heard that the Dalai Lama is coming for a visit this year. You didn't mention that at our first meeting."

"Yes, we are hosting His Holiness for teachings and the Kalachakra ceremony."

"I did read about *that* in the paper. Pretty big deal. Tibetan art exhibition, public teaching in Central Park at the invitation of Richard Gere. They're calling it the Year of Tibet. Movie stars, rock stars, a sit down with President Bush . . . That's a pretty big spotlight on your political plight. But you didn't think it was worth mentioning any of that when you hired me?"

"Politics and publicity are not my concern."

"But why involve Tibetans in a serial murder case with all of that going on? You must know that the blowback could jeopardize everything."

"Stopping the killing is my first concern." Is that an edge of anger in his voice?

"If you believe in protector demons, maybe the killing is to protect you . . . or His Holiness."

"That is no justification."

"You're not telling me everything."

To this he says nothing. I've had enough doublespeak and evasion, enough games. I throw my hands up and turn toward the door.

"I quit," I announce in a tone loud enough to echo. As the words leave my mouth something flashes past my head and a sound like a hammer striking a nail punctuates my reverberating declaration. I follow the line of the gold blur and see a *dorje*, a ritual tool, embedded in the soft wood of a painted pillar a few feet ahead of me at eye level.

And that's when shit gets weird.

The air around the point of impact ripples like water, prismatic waves breaking over me in concentric circles. Time stops and I'm tripping. Everything—the walls, the polished floorboards, even my hands in front of me—sparkles like a thin veil stretched over a scintillating light. It only lasts for the beat it takes me to draw a breath, but time belongs to another realm. We stand outside of time, the Rinpoche, the *dorje*, and myself, blazing in a fractured fragment of infinity, my eyes streaming tears of light, and then the *dorje* falls to the floor with a *thunk*.

Did it really stick in the wood for a second, like a crossbow bolt, or did it just hit the pillar and fall, the moment of impact stretched by whatever illusion the monk conjured?

I don't know. My skin prickles.

What *was* that? A trick, a hallucination?

It was the shattering of the mental constructs that obscure absolute reality.

Is that *his* voice in my head or mine?

I reach out and touch the pitted wood of the pillar with my fingertips and realize that I'm crying. I'm crying, and all I've lost is something I never had until a second ago. A glimpse. *For* a second. For an eternity.

I can't turn and look at him.

I swallow and sniffle, get a grip on myself.

"What did you say, Detective?" Rinpoche asks. His voice is soft but it carries.

"I'll keep looking."

"Good, good. Time is precious."

14

I'M STILL REELING when a young monk hands me an envelope stuffed with cash to cover my expenses and ushers me out the side door. I check for the undercover cop at the corner. When I don't see him, I stuff the envelope into my jacket pocket and join the flow of pedestrians. Everything still looks a little brighter, more vibrant than usual, and one of the first things I see on the street is Jigme Rinpoche's face again, smiling at me from a poster taped to an electrical box. Apparently he's giving a public talk on mindfulness and compassion at the Union Square Theater on February 23rd. My step falters as I read the flyer, and for a moment I consider turning tail and marching back into the dharma center to ask him why he's appearing in public when there might be assassins prowling around. But that's Norbu's alleged concern, not his.

It's only been a couple of days but enough has happened that I bet there might be something worth hearing on the cassette recorder I tucked behind the ceiling tile in Paul Tien's office. I'm still carrying my gun from walking Gemma home last night, so there's no need to stop at *my* office, and that's good because the cops are probably waiting for me to show up there.

We still have to talk about the dead fortune-teller, after all, and that could eat up half the day.

I decide to hit the karaoke bar while the night owls are still sleeping.

To my surprise, my luck is holding out. I find the place deserted, the basement window behind the dumpster no more secure than the last time I was here. I guess no one noticed the missing booze or the signs of forced entry. Not yet, anyway. Maybe they've had other things keeping them occupied. Having done this once before, I'm inside within a minute, standing in the now familiar stock room, ears pricked. The room appears untouched since my last visit.

I slip down the hall, move the subwoofer, and climb up to remove my recorder, relay, and wires. I'm lifting the ceiling tile with my head when I hear the door slam upstairs followed by footsteps pounding across the floor.

In a split second decision, I pop the cassette out of the deck and drop it into a coat pocket, then stuff the rest of the gear and wires back into the ceiling and drop the tile. The tape is small enough that it might go unnoticed if they frisk me, but if they find the recorder, it's game over. I drag the subwoofer back to where it belongs, still thinking about not drawing attention to the recorder but probably costing myself the time I need to get my ass down the hall and out the window before the three bears find Goldilocks in the just right bed.

I make it down the hall to the drumming of shoes on the stairs, and I'm through the stock room with my head and torso half out the window when someone seizes my legs. I was expecting this so I go with it, giving up some ground right away to loosen the tension and hopefully help my attacker lose balance. It doesn't work as well as I'd like, but it buys me the opportunity to recoil and kick out with some force, earning a grunt loud enough to reach my ears up at ground level in the alley.

Then the hands are on me again, one on each leg, pulling my pants down as I squirm up and out. I land a flailing kick that dislodges a hand, but my assailant scrabbles for my shoes and gets them off. I'm guessing this is to slow my escape if I make it out onto the street, but then my balls light up with searing pain as the toe of my own shoe is slammed into my groin. Like I'm kicking myself in the nuts. Holy mother. As the flare of pain dims to a deep throb, I recall that I heard at least two men pounding down the stairs toward the stockroom, but only one seems to be grappling with my lower half. Which means . . .

A boot comes around the dumpster and kicks me hard in the face. I see it just in time to tuck my chin and take it on the nose—I can't afford dental work. My elbows are braced in the window frame, but I raise my forearm to block my face. It doesn't make much difference. The next kick just drives the back of my hand into my crushed nose and sends fire up between my eyes. Add a broken finger to my tab. I'm still kicking at the guy downstairs, harder now that I'm in pain. I manage to shake him and scramble up onto the pavement, crawling like a soldier under razor wire, my nose gushing blood between my hands.

The drops are bright red against the dark stones in the pavement and the gray circles of ancient chewing gum forever melded to it. What the hell's wrong with me? Why am I studying the ground? It's the heightened reality that opened up for me in the shrine room, still lingering in my system like a residual drug. Everything is so sharp. But that happens in battle, too. And this *is* battle. I look up at my assailant just in time to catch his boot between my forearms. A shock of pain shoots through my body all the way to my tailbone.

I lurch to my feet and get my first good look at the guy in the boots. Henry Lao. Paul Tien's motherless lieutenant. Thought those boots looked familiar.

The goon downstairs isn't climbing through the window after me, so he's gotta be on his way through the building. I can't let this turn into a two-on-one. Henry swings at me. I block it. His fist is heavy, like he's holding a roll of quarters or a piece of iron pipe. I try to punch him in the gut, knock the wind out of him, but he's too fast. He sidesteps around me and I lose my balance, which he exploits immediately, slamming me into the side of the dumpster, head first. The metal clangs and my vision stutters.

I shove my throbbing right hand inside my jacket and fumble for the butt of my gun, my fingers slick with blood—must've touched my face. And then he's got me by the collar, ringing the dumpster like a bell with me and I can see every rusty scratch, smell every scrap of rotting food.

For a fleeting second, my thoughts are as clear as my adrenaline-laced vision, and I wonder: does he know I visited his mother, or is he just taking it all out on me?

He answers the question without my needing to ask it, which is good because I can't draw enough breath to talk. "Who are you, motherfucker? Who are you?"

But he doesn't give me time to answer, just keeps slamming me and asking. And then there are more hands on me, pinning my arms back until they almost pop out of the sockets. If there was a moment when I might have curled my crooked fingers around the smooth grip of my trusty 1911, it has officially passed.

Goon Number Two swings me around so Henry Lao can work on me. Or search me. And now I'm thinking more about the cassette tape than the gun. Whether it's already crushed or about to be found, I'm looking at a total loss. And if it's found . . . well, I can easily picture myself back in that basement storeroom, duct taped to a folding chair while these Ghosts go to work on me with the soldering iron I saw on the bench.

My sensory acuity is swinging the other way now, losing clarity, downgraded to dull throbbing and warbling, like a tape that's been recorded over one too many times.

I have to do something. Make a play. Distract or confuse them to pause the violence.

"Henry," I say. It comes out sounding funny with my nose crushed, but it must be clear enough. I can tell by the look on his face: a squinty, puzzled scowl.

"You know me?"

I can tell he's about to slip back into his who-the-fuck-are-you punching loop, so I fill the space: "Lily's son." And maybe that's a mistake because his lip curls up.

"You get that from TV?"

I shake my head, spit blood. "She read my fortune."

"Yeah? So then you know you're gonna die."

I manage to smile. Must be quite a sight with blood on my teeth. He almost looks repulsed. I laugh and say,

"We're *all* gonna die." Maybe these monks are getting under my skin. I'm feeling existential. And it does the trick. For a second, Henry Lao doesn't know what to say, but he doesn't hit me, either, so that's good. But I'm fading fast.

Goon Number Two says something in Mandarin. Whatever it is, it has the urgency of argument. Maybe he's telling the newly minted orphan to cool it and not kill me. Maybe I'm a cop, and anyway Tien will want answers from me, not a body to dispose of. Just a guess.

Time to seize the day. I stomp on Goon Number Two's foot. His grip on my arms goes slack long enough for me to lunge forward and headbutt Lao. In the mayhem that follows, I spin free and draw my gun. Someone's shouting from a window or a fire escape and footsteps are thwacking down the alley, slapping echoes off the bricks, and I don't know which way to turn until the baseball bat connects with my temple and the gun goes off.

15

As I regain consciousness, my head wrapped tight in a bandage, my nose taped up and throbbing through the haze of pain medication dripping into my vein, I realize it's my lucky day.

Not because I'm still alive.

Not because it could be worse.

It's because of the kid. He's the first thing I see as I take in the room. I can't see my roommate, don't know what particular brand of suffering he or she is afflicted with because of the drawn curtain between our beds. I hear the murmur of conversation drifting through that curtain and see a middle-aged woman in slacks and a sweater standing at the edge of the curtain with her hand on a little girl's shoulder, and the shadow of what might be a man beside the bed. But none of them catch my eye like the acne stricken adolescent boy hanging out by the door. He has headphones around his neck and a Walkman in his hand.

Thankfully, it doesn't hurt to turn my head. I look around my side of the room and spot my stained army jacket hanging on a hook. My clothes are folded in a neat pile on a molded plastic chair at the foot of the bed beside it.

I sit up and the room tilts. I lay back, take a breath, and feel around for the control to elevate the bed into the upright position.

The kid looks over at the sound of it, and I smile at him, hoping I don't look too creepy. I wave him over. His response is to stare at his bedridden relative, who just a minute ago was boring the bejesus out of him, and pretend not to see me.

I'd really rather not use my voice; it would likely get the attention of his parents. They probably wouldn't mind him doing me the *first* favor I'm gonna ask for, but they might frown upon the second. So I wave again and give him a *psst!*

He looks up and I flap my fingers: come here. He takes a few tentative steps over to my side of the room, then shoots a glance at his parents who apparently aren't paying any attention to their wandering eldest.

"Would you hand me my jacket, please?"

He looks relieved by the simplicity of the request and I'm glad I didn't lead with, "Wanna make an easy twenty bucks?"

He lays the jacket on top of the blanket covering my legs. I put a hand on his forearm before he can retreat.

"Hang on a sec."

I dig through the pockets with my clumsy left hand (my right is bandaged and swollen, but there are no splints on my fingers). My gun and holster are probably in a locker somewhere, so I'm amazed to find the undamaged cassette tape in an inner pocket with my wallet.

I hold the tape and a twenty dollar bill up for the kid to see. "Can I rent your Walkman?"

He looks skeptical.

I take another twenty from the wallet—it's swollen with bills from the Rinpoche, but at this rate it won't be for long. "You gonna be here a little while?"

The kid looks toward his family, then nods at me.

"You're a real talker, huh? How long, you think? An hour?"

The kid shrugs. "They're waiting for test results and to see the doctor."

I pass him both bills and my tape. He swaps it for his and hands the deck over to me with the headphones, still reluctant in spite of the easy cash.

"Relax. I don't have cooties. And do I look like I'm going anywhere?"

"Guess not. Can you even fit the earphones on over your bandages?"

"I'll work it out. Now scoot."

He seems to agree that we're flirting with parental interest and withdraws, pocketing the money before he clears the curtain.

I'm on an expensive meter here, in danger of the clock running out, so I fast-forward through the calls, sampling bits and pieces, listening for pauses in the high pitched squeal every time I hold my finger on the button to find the next call. Most of them are short. Tien placing orders with karaoke CD and beverage distributors. Some of these short business calls are conducted with code words for illicit products the Ghost Shadows deal in. Drugs and untaxed cigarettes. The conversations shift in and out of English. I can't make out the Mandarin bits, but nothing in English sounds like people talking about murders or hit contracts. Of course, I'm not catching every minute of every call, rushed as I am.

The only conversation in which I catch references to the Chinatown Monster is with a girlfriend he's trying to calm down, but if he knows more than the media and the police, he doesn't give it up to reassure her. She's not the only girlfriend he talks to, either, but unlike my usual gig, that ain't what I'm looking for.

The kid beyond the curtain is giving me anxious looks. How long have I had his machine? Twenty minutes?

I fast forward for longer stretches, skipping over God knows what. I'm looking for a little luck here. I don't know if I killed a man out there in the alley. I don't know when the cops will visit me in this bed. But I've been lucky so far. Lucky enough to start believing in luck, to get superstitious about it. I mean Christ, I woke up looking at a kid with a Walkman and the tape was still in my jacket. Did the old man somehow bless me with a run of luck when he threw that little ritual scepter into the pillar and hit me with the rainbow wave? And if so, could it be that a little residual luck is still in my system like a spiritual hangover?

On the other hand, I just had the shit kicked out of me. How lucky is that?

I've been lightly thumbing the forward button, listening to the chipmunk scribbles of Tien's conversations flying by. Now I let up and press PLAY at random, a roulette wheel winding down. My luck reasserts itself enough to make me think that rather than spying on Paul Tien I should be gambling in his basement parlor today. The conversation is rattling along in Mandarin, but just when my thumb twitches towards the FF button, I hear a name I know and freeze: *Jigme Rinpoche.*

I roll it back a few seconds and listen again. No doubt about it, they've named him. And it might not mean anything, but the connection sounds weak, the other voice distant, like maybe it's coming all the way from China, and I don't need a translator to tell me that an ex-PLA hard case getting a call from China about a prominent Tibetan leader in New York is, well, not regarding a flower delivery.

I click off the tape and pop it out without rewinding. I want to keep it right at that location for when I can get a translation. For now, I slip the cassette under my pillow. The kid is already approaching my bed to get his Walkman back. His family is still oblivious to our interaction, and before I can hand it over they're distracted by two new arrivals: Detectives Chen and Grolnic.

I suffer a moment of indecision in which I almost slip the cassette deck under my blanket. But the kid's been jittery from the get go and I probably can't expect discretion from him in front of the cops. Another part of me is tempted to just hand the machine and tape over to Chen and ask him how good his Mandarin is. If there's evidence of a murder plot on that tape, why not let the police intervene at this point? I've been paid something for my part, and they're better qualified to offer protection.

Two things prevent me from doing that:

1. I obtained this tip—which is so far just a name and a hunch—by B&E and illegal wiretapping.
2. I haven't forgotten that these bastards held me by my ankles from a rooftop. They're not getting anything for free.

So I hand the kid his Walkman and tell him thanks.

"Thanks for what?" Benny Chen asks, pulling up a chair and straddling it beside my bed.

"He loaned me his radio to check the score of the Rangers game."

Chen nods at a corner of the ceiling. "You got a TV right there."

I gape at it. "Well I'll be dipped. I'm a little out of it, fellas. Just came around. Haven't even seen a nurse yet."

The detectives don't seem to have any scruples about questioning me without my doctor's consent. Grolnic leans against the counter by the sink, arms folded above his paunch. "We just have a few questions for you, Miles. Then we'll let you get some rest."

I pick up the bed control and press the call button for a nurse. I didn't want one trying to shine a light in my eyes while I was listening to the tape, but now I'd like one pronto. I hope she's a hard ass. They probably slipped past her to get in.

"You really did a number on those gangbangers," Chen says.

"How bad? Anybody dead?"

"Not yet, but they're both here in the hospital. The one you shot took it in the thigh. He'll be okay. The one you beat the crap out of is in critical. You take the ribbon for Best in Show, even with your nose more crooked than it already was."

"I didn't beat *anybody* up. They beat *me*. My gun discharged when one of 'em brained me with a bat or a pipe or some damned thing."

Chen's eyebrows go up in polite disbelief.

"What?"

145

"Accidental discharge. That's your story. Not self defense?"

"Yeah."

"Doesn't matter, you know. He lived. You have a concealed carry permit, and any judge would say you were within your rights if you feared for your life. But pistol-whipping the unarmed guy to a pulp after shooting the one with the bat . . . that's more problematic. Especially if he doesn't come out of his coma. Or expires in the night."

"Coma? What are you playing at, Chen? I didn't even get a punch in."

He leans forward, crossing his arms on the chair back and resting his chin on them. "Why are you doing this, Miles? There were witnesses."

"I blacked out when the third guy hit me with the bat. I didn't even see him. You're telling me I went to town on somebody after blacking out. That what you're telling me?"

Chen doesn't answer. Grolnic clears his throat and takes a different tack. "What were you doing there?"

I notice the question isn't *what were you doing breaking into a karaoke bar?* Maybe my assailants left that part out. Don't want the cops looking into Tien's operation too closely.

"It's my neighborhood."

"I've been trying to find you since our last chat," Chen says. "Did you go back to see the fortune teller again?"

"No."

"And yet, the day after we find her murdered, you get into a brawl with her son. Where did you sleep last night?"

"With a friend."

"She have a name?"

"Not one I'd care to share."

"Why not?" He's had enough of my bullshit and his frustration is music to my ears.

"Maybe she's married."

Chen scoffs. "I don't know who you're protecting, Landry, but I will find out and when I do, you will have your license revoked for obstruction."

Heat rises in me at that, but I count and regulate my breathing like Gemma showed me, and damned if it doesn't work.

Grolnic lays a briefcase on the counter beside the sink, pops the latches, and digs through contents I can't see from the bed. "In your visits to the dharma center, have you seen anything like this?" he asks, handing me an 8x10 photo and studying what he can see of my face through the bandages for a reaction.

It's a grainy black and white printout taken from a high vantage point, a security camera in a corner of The Dancing Crane. It takes me a minute to recognize the beaded curtain. It's parted and a dark figure is stepping through. He's mostly shadow, possibly cloaked, but what stands out is the shaggy mane of black hair from which long horns curl upward.

My arms ripple with gooseflesh.

"Do the monks use animal masks like this in their ceremonies?" Grolnic asks.

I can't help wondering if it *is* a mask, but that's crazy thinking. Painkillers softening my rational mind. I clear my throat. "I'm sure they'd show you around, but no, I didn't see any masks."

Is that the octagonal mirror on the wall that I see a

fragment of through the parted curtain? The freeze frame is too noisy to say for sure, and now the photo is gone, swept back into the briefcase as the nurse enters the room. She shoos the flies away so the doc can have a look at the sorry sack of shit they've been buzzing around. On the way out the door, Chen tells me we're not finished. Like he's on TV. I'm just glad he didn't ask me for the score of the game.

16

They won't release me until the following day. The thought of the deductible makes my head hurt even more than the beating I took, but they want to monitor me for swelling of the brain. It's the first time I've ever been afraid of my brain getting too big. Mostly I sleep and wish I could borrow another Walkman, but no opportunity presents for that. Maybe my luck has dried up, or I've pissed it all out on one of my unsteady trips to the bathroom.

Eventually I put the cassette out of mind. Not like I can translate what's on it, anyway. All I've got is a name and a vague memory of adjacent words I don't understand.

But after stewing over it for a while, I realize that's not entirely true. I can *count* in Chinese, and I might have recognized a number. In fact, I'm pretty sure Paul Tien said the number *er shi san* in the same sentence as Rinpoche's name. Twenty-three.

The date when Jigme Rinpoche is giving a public talk at the Union Square Theater. Saturday night.

It's something. It's better than nothing. And it's all I have to go on.

That gives me one day to mend, and knowing that, I'm able to shake off some of the restlessness and relax.

I know I need sleep to heal, but I ring for the nurse, worried that if I drift off now, my bruised melon might not retain the revelation. When she shows up, I borrow her pen and jot the number on the inside of my wrist. I'm out before she clicks the nib back into the barrel.

◆━━◆━━◆

Saturday night comes too soon and nothing about my ugly mug—yellow, purple, and crusted with scabs—is going to blend in at a theater full of Manhattan mahasattvas. Knowing this, I haven't even bought a ticket to Jigme Rinpoche's lecture. I pass the afternoon with busywork just to try and take the edge off. I clean my gun and polish my shoes. I eat a bowl of Ramen with a fried egg on top. Night falls. On my way out the door, I almost call and ask Norbu to put me on the guest list. No. Paul Tien is a seasoned pro, not some second generation banger. His handlers might like the idea of a public display and the pall of fear it would cast over the Tibetan community, but he isn't going to risk doing the hit sniper style in a crowded theater with limited exits.

A voice in the back of my head tells me not to take too much for granted. *All you have is a number that might not even be a date.* I put my hat on to muffle that voice. It's time to trust my instincts and follow the scent I've caught. Time to hunt the hunter.

I take a cab to Union Square and hang around on the corner where I can watch people exiting the subway and also maintain lines of sight down East 17th and Union Square East. Paul Tien has a certain bearing about him, a recognizable gait, like he's part bear, and I'm scanning for it. Tonight the streets are thick with students and hipsters. A predator should stand out. There's no shortage of monks making their way to the theater, and many of them are stocky young men with the buzz cut Tien favors, but their maroon robes make them easy to filter out.

There's a line down the block from the ticket window, and I have to admit, I'm a little awestruck that a geriatric Asian philosopher is drawing what looks like an art rock crowd. And he's not even the Dalai Lama. I guess Tibet is hotter than I realized right now, what with the Beastie Boys rapping about it and Richard Gere wrapping it around him like a shawl. Neither is on tonight's bill, but squinting at the marquee, I see that something called "The Flaming Lips" is the opening act. Sounds like a circus. I picture a Tibetan version of fire eating sword swallowers.

At 6:45, the line starts moving. I cross the street and wander down the line of ticket holders, scanning for Chinese faces, but it's almost all white folks and Tibetans. Nobody stands out, and by the time the last few college kids pour into the lobby, I'm feeling exposed. I've done a couple of laps of the street. Now I keep walking in the direction I'm headed, back toward the park, with my hat brim low, thinking maybe I shouldn't have worn it at all. It stands out, but I can't bring myself to toss it before stepping into the alley that runs between the building that houses the theater and the red brick apartments looming over the bodegas next door.

Oddly, I feel even more exposed in the alley. To anyone lurking in the deep shadows here, I'm backlit by street lamps and passing cars. And by anyone, I mean Paul Tien. I can tell he's here, can taste the threat like heat lightning gathering in the atmosphere on a summer's day.

My bandaged hand slips into my jacket pocket, crooked fingers curling around the grip of my gun. Even that small gesture is enough to provoke a warning signal. A red laser dot glides across my chest and hovers over my heart like a wasp. I stop dead in my tracks and look up at the switchback cascade of fire escapes clinging to the bricks. There's a figure hunched on the lowest landing, a glint of glass where an eye should be. The red thread connecting us twinkles in and out of existence on the dust and ice flecks in the dry air.

"Thought you might turn up," he says, and it's the same voice I heard on the phone recordings. "I should drop you where you stand. Two for the price of one."

"Go for it," I tell him. My heart goes cold under the jittery red dot. Actually, as targeting lasers go, it's exhibiting the bare minimum in jitters. Paul Tien has a steady hand. At least I know I won't suffer if he commits to it.

Maybe half a minute passes between us before I speak again. "I'm guessing you don't have a silencer on that thing with the other fancy accessories, or you would have done me already."

Is that a laugh I hear fluttering down like feathers? "You ever use one?" he asks me.

"No."

"They don't work as well as on TV."

"That right?"

"What do you want, Landry?"

I think about it. "I want you to climb down that ladder and go home. Leave my client alone."

"Your client. So you're a professional, like me. The old monk *hired* you to hunt my guys?"

"*They* attacked *me*. I just defended myself."

"Bullshit. You're an assassin."

I laugh. "You're the one on a fire escape with a bead on me."

"Listen. You're going to take that gun out of your pocket real slow, two fingers on the grip. And you're gonna put it on the ground and step back with your hands up. Got it? Go."

I do as he says. He watches me, but his eyes also tick to what I figure has to be the stage door. When I've stepped back from the gun, he comes down the ladder one handed, the red dot jumping around my jacket with each rung. He walks toward me, kicks my gun aside.

"Get on your knees," Tien says. "Hands behind your head."

Again, I obey. He moves around me to where he can keep the door in his sights.

"You got more than one boss? You working for a rival tong on the side?" He knocks my hat off and I feel cold steel clip the back of my head. "Don't lie."

"Just the monks."

"Then why'd you kill Sammy Fong?"

"I didn't."

"I said don't fucking lie! You strung him up. One of my boys watched you do it."

"Then he's lying."

"He wasn't the first, either. Didn't know who you were until we caught you breaking into my bar. Man, you are one bold son-of-a-bitch, I'll give you that. I was tempted to snuff you in your hospital bed, but then I'd never know who hired you. So who hired you, Landry? Who you been killing Chinese for?"

"I don't know what you're talking about."

"Not just Ghosts. The fortune-teller, too. Why her? Because her son's a Ghost?"

"The monks hired me—

Flashes of ceremonial blades, my face in a broken mirror, hemp rope, blood.

—to find out who the Chinatown Monster is."

He laughs again. My legs are cramping, my feet going numb from kneeling. "You crazy mother fucker. You *are* the Monster."

There's a squeal of metal on metal as the stage door opens and it's the red dot that saves my life. I see it gliding up the door as it opens, and that means it's not on my head. A maroon robe appears in a wedge of yellow light and then I'm launching myself upward, driving an elbow into Tien, and knocking him to the pavement with a grunt.

The gun goes off and the monk in the doorway flinches at a shard of brick. Norbu. I catch sight of him hunching and scurrying out of the line of fire, but then I can't see shit, tangled up in Tien's limbs and coat as we grapple. I knee him in the groin, claw at his face, my head flooded with a horror show of butchered limbs, coarse black fur, and curved white horns. Then I'm growling and biting Tien's ear and he's screaming and my claws are wrapped around his wrist, struggling to point the gun he's holding away from the door where Jigme Rinpoche is stepping through.

The gun discharges again and a bullet bores into the hollow of my shoulder, a molten drop of flame. I crush his hand in mine and it goes off again. I feel the recoil in my bones. Tien's fingers go slack, the gun clatters to the pavement, and I'm plunged into memory's pool, swimming in blood—mine, the assassin's, and all the gallons I've ever spilled. In Chinatown, Panama, Tibet. In this life and countless others from beginningless time.

17

I WAS BORN in the Year of the Ox.

That's my first thought when I wake up in the hospital again. The hospital where I was born. Mount Sinai. My next thought is that the confrontation with Paul Tien in the alley was a bad dream, that I'm still here from getting beaten by his goons; I never left.

No. The room might look the same, but it's different. Different wounds, too. And the first thought nags at me again before I can distract myself from it, like it's been waiting by the bedside for me to wake up so it can poke my throbbing shoulder and whisper in my ear, demanding my attention.

Your birthday is in January. Chinese New Year changes dates with the lunar cycle but it always comes later than the 14th. Often as late as February. You're not a tiger, you're an ox.

Someone clears his throat. I turn my head to find Joe Navarro and Benny Chen staring at me.

"Why?" Chen asks. Navarro doesn't speak, but his eyes tell me everything. A soldier's eyes, empty of anger and denial, of everything but grief. They know what I've done. And without Joe saying a word, I know he's thinking about the repeal of the death penalty in

New York, thinking about how I made my own bed, but at least he's not sending me to the chair.

"We searched your building, your apartment, your office," Chen says. "Found the box of secrets you kept in your safe. A shaggy mask with horns; an antique Tibetan flaying knife with a quartz blade; a steel *khukuri* for carving through gristle; a silver-plated skull cap with traces of your saliva and David Yu's blood. Did you drink his blood from it after you butchered him, you sick son-of-a-bitch?"

He's holding a little black box with a glowing red light. Now I'll be the one on tape if I talk. "We have everything we need to convict," Chen says, "but it'd be nice to have motive, too."

I listen to the beeping of the medical equipment, the squeaking of shoes on the tiles in the corridor beyond the curtain. I listen to the sound of my breathing.

"Going ape isn't unheard of for a vet," Joe says, "but the racial profiling, the ritual paraphernalia . . . that's messed up."

"That's some serial killer shit," Chen says.

Joe rubs his palms over his khakis and exhales heavily. He looks up at the ceiling and asks, "Why, Miles? What drove you to do it?"

The drugs are pulling me back down into the dark and my voice sounds like someone else's when I answer: "Poison prayer got stuck in my mind, like a bad seed caught in a wheel . . . dropped here and took root."

Joe snaps his fingers near my closed eyes.

I'm falling through drops of flame.

"Miles. You're not making sense. What made you do it?"

"Snow in my bones . . . beast in my blood . . . wind in my heart."

18

I'M LESS THAN a year into a life sentence at Great Meadow Correctional in Comstock, NY. Always thought I'd like to retire upstate someday, but for all I see of the outside, I may as well be in China. Paul Tien is back on the street, but Joe says the Fifth Precinct is keeping tabs on him. In October, the Dalai Lama's visit to the Big Apple went off without a hitch, and things have settled down again for the monks of the Diamond Path Dharma Center. They have more time now for general meditation classes, hospital chaplaincy, and prison ministry visits.

Far as I know, I'm the only Buddhist currently in residence. I took the refuge vows from Jigme Rinpoche the first time he visited me. Not monastic vows, not yet, just your garden variety vows to seek refuge in the three jewels: the Buddha, the Dharma, and the Sangha. But I already have a pretty monkish haircut, so who knows? I may get there. I've got time.

For a while there, I thought my guru might be joining me full time. The police took a close look at Jigme and Norbu while I was awaiting trial, investigating whether they might be accessories to the Chinatown Monster spree, guilty of conspiracy to murder, despite my statement that I acted alone.

Who could blame them for pursuing it? The idea that I was hired to find a reincarnation, to find myself in fact, would not compute in a cop's brain. And it begged the question of why—if Jigme knew I was the killer—he didn't turn me in but instead sent me out stalking the gangland where the victims were turning up.

It's a good question. One he hasn't answered for me yet. I plan to ask him again today.

The guards lead me into the visitor's room, just a table and a couple of chairs. Rinpoche is seated. He never quite looks comfortable in a chair. I wish we could have meditation cushions. Most of our time together so far has been spent on meditation instruction. I practice a lot. I won't say it's easy, but like anything, the more you do it . . .

My practice makes me something of a curiosity in here, where most guys, if they believe in anything, just pray. I get asked about it. One guy—this roid head named Dave Rizzo who used to be a contract killer—claimed he tried meditation a few times when he was taking karate, but gave it up when it didn't do anything for him. I told him that's like lifting weights a few times and then giving it up because it didn't do anything for you. You develop the mental muscle, the concentration, through daily practice.

That's what Rinpoche tells me, anyway.

If it does what he promises and pacifies the anger blowing through me like a storm . . . well, then I might just make it through this. I don't have too many other choices.

I approach Jigme and offer my hand for a supervised handshake. I feel bad when he rises to greet me, but he waves off my protest, takes my fingers, and gives them a gentle squeeze, like he did the first time we met. He looks arthritic settling back into the chair, but the same old joyous light I've always seen in his eyes is still there. Maybe more, now that the monster he felt responsible for is safely caged.

I sit and fold my hands on the table, attentive.

"How are you?" he asks.

I tell him I'm okay and ask after Norbu.

"Good, good."

"No lingering problems from the gunshot wound?"

"Not so much. He had a good doctor."

"And a good lawyer."

Rinpoche laughs. "Just some scar tissue in the stomach they have to watch."

"Tell him I said hello."

"Okay. How is your practice?"

"It's going okay, I guess. I still have trouble controlling my rage, but when I'm sitting my mind is less restless, more stable."

He nods, looks around. "Prison is a little bit like a monastery. Not many distractions. A serious practitioner could accomplish much in a single lifetime."

That's all I have now—a lifetime without distraction. Maybe there's another kind of freedom in this loss of freedom. When all of the lesser life choices have been taken away from you, why not shoot for enlightenment?

"Any visions or dreams?" he asks.

He and I have talked before about not placing too much importance on dreams, visions, or memories, about the illusory nature of anything that isn't the living reality of the moment. But he still wants me to observe whatever may arise as I settle my mind.

"I've had a few . . . I don't know, memories? When I'm sitting. They *feel* like memories. I don't know."

"Of the murders?"

"Some. And of Tibet, maybe? Mostly just glimpses. Images. We watched an old black and white movie last month, *The Naked City*. The climax takes place on the Williamsburg Bridge. I'd never seen the film before, but watching it gave me this weird sensation . . . I could swear I had a memory of watching it with a group of Tibetan freedom fighters at a training camp in Colorado. Like it was the thing that made Dorje want to see New York. I don't know, but I think it could be why he reincarnated here: a fascination with a faraway place. A romantic notion of a mythical kingdom. Like how some Americans feel about Tibet. Do you think that's possible?"

"Could be. Maybe these are memories. Maybe imagination. It's okay. Let them come, let them go. Do not grasp at them."

We sit in silence for a while. Me in plain blue prison pajamas, my teacher in his robes. The guards shift. Silence makes them restless, but I'm starting to think I get more out of his presence when we're just sitting together than I do from trying to talk to him about it all. He has sent me some books to study, and I know there will be days ahead, hopefully years, when we will spend these sessions analyzing and debating commentaries on the scriptures, but for now his presence alone means more to me. Until I remember the question that keeps nagging me.

"If you saw Dorje Tsering in me, if you knew I was

the monster . . . why didn't you tell me? Why the game? Why didn't you stop me sooner?"

"If I told you, you would have believed me?"

"No."

"The police? They would believe?"

"Of course not."

"You had to find him in you. Same with Buddha."

I let this sink in while he places a small cardboard box on the table. Whatever's inside must have passed inspection.

"A gift for you."

"I still feel the anger," I say, not acknowledging the box until he acknowledges more of my question, more of my worry. "People in here test me, make me want to lash out. Guards, inmates."

Rinpoche pats the little box and says, "Practice."

I slide it toward me and lift the white cardboard lid. There's a black onyx *mala* coiled on a cotton square. I pick it up and thumb the smooth beads. The clacking sound is familiar, soothing.

"I blessed it," Rinpoche says. "Practice *Om mani padme hum*. Compassion Buddha mantra."

"This isn't the one you showed me when we first met. The one that belonged to Dorje Tsering."

A wisp of a smile. "The prison only allows black prayer beads. But even if there was no rule, I would give you new. You are a different man."

I draw a deep shuddering breath to get a handle on the emotion welling up in me. A different man from Dorje Tsering. I want that to be true. And as Rinpoche squeezes my hand with the *mala* in it and rises from his chair, I think maybe I'm a different man from Miles Landry, too. Maybe I'm not just going around in circles. Maybe these revolutions are evolution. In 1960 a monk gave up his robes and became a soldier. In 1991 a former soldier gave up his gun and took vows. Maybe all of the people I've been are beads on the same string, each unique, each flawed, each marking a breath, a prayer, a step on the path.

The End?

Not if you want to dive into more of Crystal Lake Publishing's Tales from the Darkest Depths!

Check out our amazing website and online store:
https://www.crystallakepub.com

We always have great new projects and content on the website to dive into, as well as a newsletter, behind the scenes options, social media platforms, and our very own store. If you use the IGotMyCLPBook! coupon code in the store (at the checkout), you'll get a one-time-only 50% discount on your first purchase!

We even have categories specifically for Kindle Unlimited books, non-fiction, anthologies, and others.

Acknowledgements

My sincere thanks go out to Mark Burns and Daniel Braum who read an early version of the manuscript and provided valuable feedback. Gratitude is also due to Joe Mynhardt, Renee S. DeCamillis, Ben Baldwin, and the rest of the team at Crystal Lake Publishing for doing great work to put this book in your hands in polished form. The Wind In My Heart would not exist without the kindness and support of Geshe Gendun Gyatso, my teacher in the study of Vajrayana Buddhism since 2005. Thanks also to my dear friends at the Healing Dharma Center of Newburyport and to Jabberwocky Bookshop for generously hosting our classes. Any misrepresentations of Tibetan Buddhism in the service of fiction are my responsibility alone.

About the Author

Douglas Wynne is the author of five previous novels, including *The Devil of Echo Lake*, *Steel Breeze*, and the SPECTRA Files trilogy. His short fiction has appeared in numerous anthologies and his writing workshops have been featured at genre conventions and schools throughout New England. He lives in Massachusetts with his wife and son and a houseful of animals. You can find him online at www.douglaswynne.com.

Since its founding in August 2012, Crystal Lake Publishing has quickly become one of the world's leading publishers of Dark Fiction and Horror books in print, eBook, and audio formats.

While we strive to present only the highest quality fiction and entertainment, we also endeavour to support authors along their writing journey. We offer our time and experience in non-fiction projects, as well as author mentoring and services, at competitive prices.

With several Bram Stoker Award wins and many other wins and nominations, Crystal Lake Publishing puts integrity, honor, and respect at the forefront of our publishing operations.

We strive for each book and outreach program we spearhead to not only entertain and touch or comment on issues that affect our readers, but also to strengthen and support the Dark Fiction field and its authors.

Not only do we find and publish authors we believe are destined for greatness, but we strive to work with men and woman who endeavour to be decent human beings who care more for others than themselves, while still being hard working, driven, and passionate artists and storytellers.

Crystal Lake Publishing is and will always be a beacon of what passion and dedication, combined with overwhelming teamwork and respect, can accomplish. We endeavour to know each and every one of our readers, while building personal relationships with our authors, reviewers, bloggers, podcasters, bookstores, and libraries.

We will be as trustworthy, forthright, and transparent as any business can be, while also keeping most of the headaches away from our authors, since it's our job to solve the problems so they can stay in a creative mind. Which of course also means paying our authors.

We do not just publish books, we present to you worlds within your world, doors within your mind, from talented authors who sacrifice so much for a moment of your time.

There are some amazing small presses out there, and through collaboration and open forums we will continue to support other presses in the goal of helping authors and showing the world what quality small presses are capable of accomplishing. No one wins when a small press goes down, so we will always be there to support hardworking, legitimate presses and their authors. We don't see Crystal Lake as the best press out there, but we will always strive to be the best, strive to be the most interactive and grateful, and even blessed press around. No matter what happens over time, we will also take our mission very seriously while appreciating where we are and enjoying the journey.

What do we offer our authors that they can't do for themselves through self-publishing?

We are big supporters of self-publishing (especially hybrid publishing), if done with care, patience, and planning. However, not every author has the time or inclination to do market research, advertise, and set up book launch strategies. Although a lot of authors are successful in doing it all, strong small presses will always be there for the authors who just want to do what they do best: write.

What we offer is experience, industry knowledge, contacts and trust built up over years. And due to our strong brand and trusting fanbase, every Crystal Lake Publishing book comes with weight of respect. In time our fans begin to trust our judgment and will try a new author purely based on our support of said author.

With each launch we strive to fine-tune our approach, learn from our mistakes, and increase our reach. We continue to assure our authors that we're here for them and that we'll carry the weight of the launch and dealing with third parties while they focus on their strengths—be it writing, interviews, blogs, signings, etc.

We also offer several mentoring packages to authors that include knowledge and skills they can use in both traditional and self-publishing endeavours.

We look forward to launching many new careers.

This is what we believe in. What we stand for. This will be our legacy.

Welcome to Crystal Lake Publishing—Tales from the Darkest Depths

THANK YOU FOR PURCHASING THIS BOOK

CPSIA information can be obtained
at www.ICGtesting.com
Printed in the USA
LVHW052353020321
680382LV00014B/2194

3/21